EDUCATION IN CANADA: AN OVERVIEW

Paula Dunning

*Canadian Education Association
Suite 8-200, 252 Bloor Street West,
Toronto, Ontario M5S 1V5*

1997

About the Author

Paula Dunning is a writer specializing in projects for the education sector. She is a former public school trustee and former president of the Ontario Public School Boards' Association. She also teaches a part-time writing clinic at Algoma University College in Sault Ste. Marie, Ontario.

© Canadian Education Association
Suite 8-200, 252 Bloor Street West,
Toronto, Ontario M5S 1V5

1997

ISBN: 1-896660-10-X

Cover by Lancaster & Reid Design

Printed in Canada

Publié en français sous le titre : L'éducation au Canada : vue d'ensemble

CONTENTS

Chapter 1
CANADA'S ELEMENTARY AND SECONDARY SCHOOLS

Decision-making for Canada's Public Schools	1
The Provincial Government	2
Local Government	4
The Federal Government	7
Collaboration and Co-operation	11
Paying for Public Education in Canada	12
Revenue Sources	13
Sharing the Wealth	15
Separate School Funding	17
Funding for Private and Independent Schools	18
Provincial Summaries of Governance and Finance	18
Canada's Schools: A Profile	21
The School Population	21
Graduation Rates	22
Pre-school Programs	24
School Organization	25
The School Day and School Year	25
Textbooks and Learning Materials	26
Elementary Schools	26
Secondary Schools	28
Provincial Summary of Diploma Requirements	29
Language Instruction	32
Language Programs for Immigrant Students	34
Education for Native Children	35
Special Education	38
Education or Social Service?	39
Private Schools	39
Special Subject Schools	40
Home Schooling	41
Measuring System Performance	41
Public Opinion	42
Teaching in Canada	43
The Workforce	43

Gender Issues in the Teaching Profession	44
Teacher Education	44
Working Conditions	45

Chapter 2
POST-SECONDARY EDUCATION IN CANADA

Higher Education: Investing in the Future	47
Post-secondary Education in Canada: A Short History	48
Enrolment Patterns and Program Choices	50
Native Student Participation	54
Personal Benefits of Post-Secondary Education	54
Responding to Change	55
Portability of Courses and Credits	56
Canadian Universities	57
Admission Requirements and Programs of Study	57
Language of Instruction	59
School Year	59
Tuition Fees	59
Accommodation	61
University Governance	61
New Calls for Accountability	62
Teaching in Canadian Universities	63
A Tradition of Research	63
Canada's Community College System	65
Admission Requirements and Programs of Study	66
School Year	67
Language of Instruction	67
Tuition Fees	67
Community College Governance	67
Focus on Student Learning	68
Some Highlights of Canadian Post-secondary Education	69
Co-operative Education	69
Distance Education	69
Post-secondary Education: An International Dimension	71
Paying for Post-secondary Education	72
Institutional Funding	73
Student Loans	74

Tax Supports for Post-secondary Education 75

Chapter 3
LIFELONG LEARNING: ADULT EDUCATION IN CANADA

Education for Employment 77
    Trade/Vocational and Preparatory Programs 77
    Apprenticeship Training 79
    The Canadian Labour Force Development Board 80

Creating a Learning Culture 81
    Adult Continuing Education 81
    Literacy Programs 86
    Adult Education: Changing Perspectives 87

Chapter 4
EDUCATIONAL TRENDS IN CANADA

    Greater Emphasis on Curriculum Outcomes
        and Assessment 89
    The Technology Revolution in the Classroom 91
    School-to-Work Transitions 93
    Trends in Post-secondary Education 96
    Trends in Skills Development and Training 97

USEFUL ADDRESSES

Departments of Education 99
A Few Federal Addresses 101
National Education Organizations and Associations 107

INTRODUCTION

FORMAL LEARNING OPPORTUNITIES for children and adults in Canada are available in a bewildering combination of institutions and political jurisdictions. These vary from province to province, since the Canadian federation leaves education in the hands of the ten provincial and two territorial governments. However, despite real and sometimes confusing regional differences, both educational goals and the structures responsible for meeting them are evolving in similar ways and responding to similar pressures, from Newfoundland to British Columbia to the Northwest Territories.

The following overview has been written to provide the lay person with a summary of the system's current status, its governance and funding structures, its program offerings, and its major trends.

The book is divided into three broad areas: elementary and secondary, post-secondary, and adult education. For the purposes of general discussion, these are natural divisions. From the perspective of individuals, however, the boundaries are not as clear as might be supposed. Adults do attend secondary schools; workplace training is often the first step to higher education; high school students enrol in university courses; community educators offer programs through elementary and secondary schools. The various sectors of education in Canada should be seen not as discreet units, but as pieces of a puzzle attached to one another on several surfaces, and in a variety of ways.

No social system is static — certainly not Canadian education at the end of the 20th century. The statistics used in this volume are the most current available at the time of writing. They should, however, be read as indicators of general trends or illustrations of specific points, since such figures are often out of date by the time they are released, and only become more so with the passage of time. Likewise, legislative changes are affecting education in every province. No attempt to capture the status of education across the country can be more than a snapshot of a moving landscape. But, like a snapshot, it can point to significant features and reveal which way the wind is blowing.

Paula Dunning
April 1997

Chapter 1

CANADA'S ELEMENTARY AND SECONDARY SCHOOLS

Decision-making for Canada's Public Schools

... education is an integral part of the social fabric of a nation ...[1]

THE EDUCATION of the young is essential to the health and stability of all societies. In complex industrialized nations like Canada, establishing and maintaining educational systems is a priority for governments, which are responsible for the personal well-being of their citizens and the economic well-being of their country.

Although three tiers of government participate in the delivery of elementary and secondary education in Canada, final responsibility falls squarely on the ten provinces and two territories. The *British North America Act* of 1867, and its successor, the *Constitution Act* of 1982, give provincial governments the legal, administrative and financial responsibility for elementary and secondary education. All of the provincial educational systems have similar structures and objectives, but they do reflect historical differences in governance, finance, and educational priorities. Canada's level of decentralization in the important area of education is probably unique in the world.

---

[1] Francis R. Whyte, "Tidy Minds and the National Education Perspective," *Is There a National Role in Education?* (Toronto: Canadian Education Association and Canadian Society for the Study of Education, 1994), p 11.

The Provincial Government

In each province, an act of the legislature, usually called the *Schools Act* or the *Education Act*, contains the government policies relating to education. In some provinces, the Department or Ministry of Education also includes colleges, universities, and/or training. The Department of Education is led by a Minister of Education, who is an elected member of the provincial legislature. He or she is responsible for administering the *Education Act* or *Schools Act*, introducing legislative changes, and implementing such changes.

The Minister delegates responsibility for policy development and day-to-day management of the department to a senior civil servant, the deputy minister. The deputy advises the minister, supervises the activities of the department, enforces regulations, and provides continuity in educational policy.

Provincial departments of education are responsible for the supervision of elementary and secondary schools; the design and distribution of curriculum materials; structures for school governance and administration; methods of assessment and the standards for student testing; new courses and textbooks; school funding policies and levels; regulations for trustees and education officials of school boards, principals and teachers; research; support services such as libraries and transportation; and, in most provinces, teacher certification.

Most provincial initiatives in education focus on the quality and efficiency of the system. Common themes include educational standards, basic skills, measuring and reporting results, learning technologies, improving core curriculum, reducing drop-out rates, involving parents, co-op education and vocational education.[2] Recently, most provinces have been engaged in extensive reforms which touch on all aspects of the school system, including curriculum, governance and financing.

Diploma Requirements and Learning Objectives

Each provincial department determines the courses and standards of achievement required for graduation from secondary school, as well as the criteria for progressing through the system.

The departments set learning objectives for core subject areas at each grade level and develop curricular responses to areas of public concern (i.e., AIDS education).

---

[2] *Ibid.*, p 16.

Curriculum Guidelines and Materials

Departments of education issue curriculum guidelines for each division or grade, and for each subject area. These guidelines provide general outlines of course content, and are usually developed by teams of educators from the elementary, secondary, and post-secondary systems, as well as departmental personnel. Detailed curriculum is then developed at the local school board, under the direction of the board's supervisory officers. Recently, there has been a move in some provinces to centralize all curriculum development, in the interest of both efficiency and consistency.

Teacher Certification

The department of education in all provinces and territories except Ontario and British Columbia grant teaching certificates to those who comply with their particular regulations. In both of those provinces, a self-regulating College of Teachers sets teacher qualifications and grants certificates. Training for elementary and secondary teachers is conducted by faculties of education within universities, which prepare students to meet the regulations of their provinces.

Setting Financial Frameworks

Provincial departments of education set the financial frameworks under which school boards operate. The majority of provinces provide most of the funding for school board operations.

Collective Bargaining

Provincial governments set the parameters for collective bargaining with teachers and other employee groups. In some provinces, all salary levels and working conditions are negotiated provincially; in some they are negotiated jointly between the province and the local board; and in some the responsibility falls entirely to the local board.

The trend to centralize more power at the provincial level has resulted in a general shift of responsibility away from boards. In New Brunswick, Prince Edward Island and Newfoundland, teachers' collective agreements are negotiated entirely between the province and the teacher unions. In Alberta, Ontario, and Manitoba, teachers negotiate at the local board level. In the other provinces (British Columbia, Saskatchewan, Quebec and Nova Scotia), teacher negotiations occur at both levels, with some items decided provincially and others locally.

When difficulties arise at the bargaining table, the usual route to agreement is through conciliation, mediation, and arbitration. Teacher strikes are permitted in Alberta, Saskatchewan, Ontario, New Brunswick, Newfoundland, the Yukon and the Northwest Territories, and in British Columbia, Quebec, and Nova Scotia on provincially negotiated items only.

Seeking Public Input

Most provincial departments of education seek public input into decision-making through task forces, advisory or review committees, parliamentary commissions, discussion papers and surveys. In some provinces, formal consultative bodies have been established to advise the minister.

Local Government

Most provinces delegate the operation of school systems to locally elected school boards of "trustees" or "commissioners." School boards have existed in what is now Canada since before Confederation. The number of boards, the size and boundaries of their districts, and the number of trustees and their duties are defined in the various *Education/School Acts*. In some provinces school boards have broad powers to tax, negotiate contracts, and make major decisions about the management of their local school systems, but in all cases they are creatures of the province and exist under legislation that defines and delegates their powers.

Some Trends in Local School Governance

In 1994, the Canadian School Boards Association identified four trends in local school governance:
- Reduction in number of school boards;
- Redefinition of school board powers and responsibilities;
- Centralization of power at the provincial/territorial level;
- Redirection of some responsibilities to school-based parent or community advisory councils.[3]

During the 1990s, most provinces reduced both the number and the powers of school boards. In 1995, New Brunswick became the first

---

[3] Canadian School Boards Association, *Who's Running our Schools? Education Governance in the 90's: A Handbook for School Trustees* (Ottawa: CSBA, 1995), p. vi.

Canadian province to eliminate school boards altogether; Prince Edward Island reduced the number of its local school boards from five to three; Alberta, British Columbia, Nova Scotia and Newfoundland have all amalgamated local boards into fewer, larger units; Quebec and Ontario are scheduled to follow suit in 1998.

Along with the trend toward larger school boards has come a parallel trend toward more centralized decision-making at the provincial level.

Mandate of School Boards

School board responsibilities include setting an annual budget; delegating responsibility for professional administration of schools; establishing policies to be implemented by local professional educators and other board staff; hiring, promoting and dismissing teachers and administrators; building schools; and purchasing supplies. In some provinces, boards are authorized to levy residential and commercial property taxes (or to requisition taxes from municipal governments) and to manage grants from the provincial department of education.

Traditionally, school boards have also been responsible for initiating local programs, like day care, breakfast programs, and adult education, and for ensuring that local priorities are reflected in curriculum and classroom activities.

Most trustees see their jobs as part-time community service, and receive a small honorarium, or a stipend for each meeting attended. In urban centres with large school populations, there has been a trend toward larger salaries for trustees: $50,000 in Toronto, $19,000 in Vancouver, $7,680 in Montreal and $6,000 in Halifax. Proposed changes in Ontario will define the trustee role as part-time, and limit all trustees (currently receiving an average of $10,000) to a maximum honorarium of $5,000.

Size and Structure of School Boards

The size of school boards varies from province to province, and within provinces. In urban areas, school boards typically cover a single city and some of the smaller communities surrounding it. In rural areas, they often cover vast areas that include many small communities. In remote northern communities, a school board may be responsible for a single school with only a few students. The number of trustees per school board is usually based on population or student enrolment, although geographic area is sometimes included in the calculation of trustee numbers.

Some provinces hold trustee elections at the same time as municipal elections; others hold them separately. The term of office is usually two or three years. In provinces with Roman Catholic (or Protestant) Separate School systems, electors vote for trustees on either the public or the separate school board in their jurisdiction.

Since the *Charter of Rights and Freedoms* came into effect in 1985, guaranteeing first-language education to French and English minorities, French-first-language school systems have slowly been emerging across the country, with elected trustees to govern the education of francophone students at the local, regional, or provincial level. Prince Edward Island and Nova Scotia have each created a single French-language board; New Brunswick (the only officially bilingual province) has had linguistically-based school boards since 1967; Ontario has had a combination of French-language boards and minority language "sections" of public and separate boards; and Manitoba, Saskatchewan and Alberta have each created regional French-language boards to provide French-language education. Reforms in Ontario will see 12 French boards in place to serve the whole province by 1998, and Quebec proposes to base school boards on language rather than religion.

Supervisory Personnel

School boards usually select their own chief supervisory officer, called a director of education or superintendent of schools, who is responsible for implementing the policies of the board, administering the school system according to the laws and regulations of the province, and delegating duties to principals and teachers. In some provinces, the Minister of Education approves the director or superintendent of schools' professional qualifications and confirms the appointment.

In small school systems, the director or superintendent of education may be the only supervisory officer. In large urban boards, a number of supervisory officers report to the director of education, and are responsible for different groups of schools or different areas of system operation or instruction.

School Councils

While funding and policy-making are becoming more centralized at the provincial level on the one hand, a number of provinces are giving more authority to parents on the other.

Individual parents and voluntary organizations like the local Parent Teacher Association (PTA) and the Canadian Home and School

Federation have always had an informal influence on elementary and secondary education at the school level, although they have been more active in some provinces and some communities than in others. To encourage public input, many school boards have routinely included parents and other members of the community on consultative committees, particularly when dealing with issues that affect the students' school life, like changes in curriculum and reorganized school structures.

Most provinces are now formalizing parental influence by introducing school or community councils. These bodies are organized at the school level, and are usually advisory to the local school board. They represent an attempt to increase parents' involvement in their children's education at the local level, and to move toward greater site-based management.

Legislation either requires or authorizes school councils in seven provinces and one territory (Nova Scotia, New Brunswick, Prince Edward Island, Quebec, Ontario, Alberta, British Columbia and the Yukon). Legislation is pending in Newfoundland and Manitoba.

For a provincial summary of governance and finance policies, please see page 18.

The Federal Government

The constitutional division of powers leaves the federal government of Canada with no formal role in the delivery of educational programs to the nation's five million elementary and secondary students. Canada has no national department of education, nor any mechanism to oversee education policy. However, the federal government is more than an outside observer of the nation's schools.

Guarantor of Minority Rights

The Constitution left the door ajar to federal involvement in elementary and secondary education just enough to protect the rights and privileges of religious and linguistic minorities.

The *British North America Act*, and subsequent *Acts* admitting new provinces to the Canadian Confederation, guaranteed that existing educational rights for religious minorities would be protected. At the time of Confederation, those minorities consisted of Protestants in Quebec and Roman Catholics in the rest of Canada. As a result, Quebec, Ontario, Alberta, Saskatchewan and the Northwest Territories operate denominational elementary and secondary school systems alongside the secular public system. Roman Catholics in these jurisdictions (and Protestants in Quebec) may send their children to publicly funded schools of their faith. Although the two systems are frequently referred to as "public" and "separate" ("dissentient" in Quebec), they are in fact two publicly supported, parallel school systems.

When Newfoundland joined Confederation in 1949, eight denominations were granted the right to operate their own schools. Some joined forces, forming four distinct school systems, which were combined into a single non-denominational public system in 1996.

By protecting denominational schools, the Constitution has tended to protect linguistically homogenous schools as well, particularly in Quebec, where Protestant school boards have primarily served the anglophone minority and Roman Catholic school boards have served the francophone majority.

In 1982, the *Canadian Charter of Rights and Freedoms* explicitly guaranteed educational rights to both French and English language minorities, extending at the same time the federal government's role as guarantor of minority rights. The intent of the *Charter* was to ensure that, wherever they live in Canada, English and French-speaking Canadians could be educated in their own language. To help the provinces meet their obligations to minority language students, the federal government provides funds to support both minority language and second official language education.

Several provincial decisions have challenged the federal government's role as protector of minority rights. In a September 1995 referendum, Newfoundlanders supported the amalgamation of their publicly-supported denominational school systems into one. The passage of a federal law was required before the province could abandon its constitutional obligation to religious minorities. By passing such a law respecting the wishes of Newfoundland's majority, the federal government opened itself to criticism for turning its back on minority religious rights.

Quebec is trying to reorganize its denominational school system along linguistic lines. This move would be consistent with societal trends in the province, but it, too, would require federal legislation to release the province from its commitment to the pre-Confederation dissentient school systems in Quebec City and on the Island of Montreal.

In his discussion of minority religious and linguistic education, Stephen Lawton points out that "... religion is declining as an organizational principle in Canadian education, while language is ascending. . ." With this observation, he raises the spectre of constitutional confusion: "The question obviously arises as to which right predominates: the right to be educated in a particular faith or in a particular language — or both?"[4]

Provider of Last Resort

The federal government assumes direct responsibility for the education of those who are beyond the boundaries of provincial jurisdiction: Native people, armed services personnel and the children of those serving overseas, and the inmates of federal penal institutions. In these cases, the relevant departments of government take responsibility for providing education.

The federal Department of Indian and Northern Affairs, itself, operates nine schools for Indian children; it funds 429 band-operated schools on reserves for Indian and Inuit children; and it pays the costs for Indian and Inuit children who attend their province's public schools. The two territories have been responsible for their own Native education programs since the late 1960s.

The Department of National Defence ensures that the children of armed forces personnel stationed overseas have access to elementary and secondary education.

Correctional Services of Canada provides education for inmates from primary through post-secondary, including vocational education and special literacy and upgrading programs.

An Indirect Role

Although the federal government's formal role in education policy is limited to the few areas noted above, it plays an indirect role through its fiscal relationship with the provinces, and through policy initiatives relating indirectly to education.

All provinces receive funds from the federal treasury as a part of a national policy to redistribute and equalize wealth among the provinces. These funds are not ear-marked for education, but they invariably influence the size of provincial education funding envelopes. In 1976, in an external review of Canadian educational policy, the Organisation for Economic Co-operation and Development (OECD) said: "Officially there is *no* federal presence in the area of educational policy... no federal authority with the word 'Education' in its title."

---

[4] Stephen B. Lawton, *Financing Canadian Education* (Toronto: Canadian Education Association, 1996), pp. 106 - 107.

However, it went on to note that there is a federal presence in education "as long as nobody calls it educational policy, and as long as there are no overt strings attached to the money coming from Ottawa."[5]

In fact, the federal government operates in many areas that are officially peripheral to education, but have a profound impact on education policy and delivery at the provincial and local levels. National policies for immigration, official languages, multiculturalism and human resources have created demand for specific programs in elementary and secondary schools, and have resulted in changes to provincial education policies.

For example, the *Canadian Multiculturalism Act* of 1988 is a federal act that officially recognizes the racial and cultural diversity of Canada. It states that all Canadians must have equal opportunity; the freedom to enjoy, enhance and share their heritage; and the right to be treated with respect. Although, strictly speaking, it is not education policy, this federal act has had a profound impact on provincial departments and ministries of education across the country. They have developed guidelines and curricula to promote multiculturalism, human rights, citizenship and cross-cultural understanding. Five provinces have introduced heritage language programs in the elementary schools to teach the children of Canadian immigrants the languages of their family's culture.

A number of national departments address the broader issues of economic development and a well-trained workforce, which lead naturally to funding for education and training programs like co-operative education and post-secondary student loan programs.

The federal departments Human Resources Development Canada and Canadian Heritage could be called Canada's *unofficial* offices of education. HRDC co-ordinates federal policies and programs related to education support, particularly for post-secondary education. Under its Learning Directorate (formerly called the Youth, Learning and Literacy Directorate), it administers the Canada Student Loans Program and the Canada Health and Social Transfer (CHST), which consolidates federal support to the provinces and territories for post-secondary education, health and social assistance. The Canadian Heritage Department administers the grants for minority language and second official language instruction at the elementary, secondary and post-secondary levels. It also funds the Summer Language Bur-

---

[5] Michael G. Fullan, *The New Meaning of Educational Change* (New York: Teacher's College Press, 1991), p. 271.

sary and the Official Language Monitor Programs (both administered by the Council of Ministers of Education, Canada). As well, Industry Canada funds the Canadian Scholarship Program to encourage studies in science and technology, the Innovators in Schools Network, and SchoolNet, an innovative federal/provincial co-operative program that links schools and other educational institutions to each other and the world via the Internet — all of which have an impact on provincial educational policy.

Collaboration and Co-operation

In the name of efficiencies, governments at all levels are looking for ways to reduce duplication and work more closely together.

At the ministry/department level, a number of provincial governments have amalgamated their departments of education with related departments to form, for example, the Department of Post-Secondary Education and Skills Training (Saskatchewan), the Ministry of Education and Training (Ontario), and the Department of Education and Culture (Nova Scotia).

Similarly, school boards have increased their level of co-operation with each other, and with other public institutions and agencies. Many school boards now co-operate in purchasing, transportation, curriculum and professional development, and other services. In some cases, these co-operative ventures have been mandated by the provinces, and have resulted in the amalgamation of several boards into a single administrative unit.

Regional Co-operation

Although curriculum development is a provincial responsibility, a number of collaborative projects are under way. The four Western Provinces (British Columbia, Alberta, Saskatchewan and Manitoba) and the two territories have developed the Western Canada Protocol, which shares mathematics and language arts curriculum. The Atlantic provinces (New Brunswick, Nova Scotia, Prince Edward Island and Newfoundland) are co-operating in the development of a common core curriculum for grades K - 12 in language arts, mathematics, science and social studies. Ontario, the Atlantic provinces and the Western provinces are working together on a K-12 pan-Canadian science framework.

Federal/Provincial Co-operation: The Council of Ministers of Education, Canada

The growing importance of education in the new economy makes elementary and secondary education a matter of national concern, even though it is not a matter of national policy. To address national priorities, national interest groups, and international social and economic trends, the provincial Ministers of Education formed the Council of Ministers of Education, Canada (CMEC) in 1967. "CMEC is the ministers' mechanism for consulting on matters of mutual interest, representing Canadian education internationally, providing liaison with various federal departments and co-operating with other national education organizations."[6] The Council has identified four critical policy areas: accessibility, quality, mobility, and relevance.[7]

In 1989, CMEC initiated the School Achievement Indicators Program (SAIP) to measure how well each province and territory's education system is performing. Tests of 13-year-olds and 16-year-olds in math, reading and writing are being administered in an ongoing cycle, and a science component was introduced in 1996. The CMEC has also been active in monitoring Canadian performance in international testing programs.

Paying for Public Education in Canada

Canadians spend between $5,000 and $7,000 per year to educate each full-time elementary and secondary school student (more in the territories). This amounts to a national expenditure of $42.6 billion, and accounts for 20% of total government spending at all levels.[8] Among the G-7 countries (Canada, France, Germany,

---

[6] Council of Ministers of Education, Canada, *The Development of Education: Report of Canada* (Toronto: CMEC, September 1996), p. 7.

[7] Canadian Education Statistics Council, *Education Indicators in Canada* (Toronto: CMEC and Statistics Canada, 1996), p. 4.

[8] Canadian Education Statistics Council, *A Statistical Portrait of Elementary and Secondary Education in Canada* (Toronto: CMEC and Statistics Canada, April 1996), pp. 71-72.

Italy, Japan, the United Kingdom and the United States), Canada continues to record the highest public investment in all levels of education relative to its economy. In 1994, Canada spent 7.3% of its GDP on education, compared to 6.8% in the United States, 5.7% in Germany, 4.9% in Japan and 4.1% in the United Kingdom.[9]

Between 1971 and 1996, expenditures on elementary and secondary education increased almost seven-fold, from $5.4 billion to $36.4 billion, with the greatest increases occurring during the late 1970s and 1980s.[10] Clearly, such rapid escalation of spending has come to a halt. During the first half of the 1990s, education costs stabilized as tax-payers protested and governments at all levels focused on deficit reduction and more efficient service delivery. In fact, the CMEC reports that *"real per student spending levels in the mid 1990s were below the peaks reached in the early 1990s for all provinces and territories. Indeed, retrenchment in elementary and secondary education has averaged about 6.5% over the past few years..."* [11]

Levels of funding for elementary and secondary education, sources of revenue to local boards, and the method of distributing it vary from province to province. In all cases, the provincial government funding frameworks are designed to ensure that adequate support for basic educational programs and services is available to local school boards.

On average, about 62% of school board expenditures goes directly to instruction — including salaries and benefits paid to educators, instructional supplies and services, desks and equipment used in instruction, and computer services relating to instruction. Other expenses break down as follows: plant operation, 9.5%; capital costs, 7.6%; other educational services, 11.2%; and transportation, 4.7%.[12]

Revenue Sources

School boards depend on two sources for more than 90 percent of their revenues: grants from provincial or territorial governments, and local property taxes levied by either the province or the local board.

---

[9] *1996: Canada at a Glance* (Ottawa: Statistics Canada, 1996). Brochure.

[10] Statistics Canada, "Education at a Glance," *Education Quarterly Review, 1996*, vol. 3, no. 4 (1996), p. 53.

[11] Council of Ministers of Education, Canada, *The Development of Education: Report of Canada, op. cit.*, p. 23.

[12] Canadian Education Statistics Council, *A Statistical Portrait, op. cit.*, p. 71.

Canada's Elementary and Secondary Schools

Sources of School Board Revenues, by Province and Territory, Canada, 1992-93

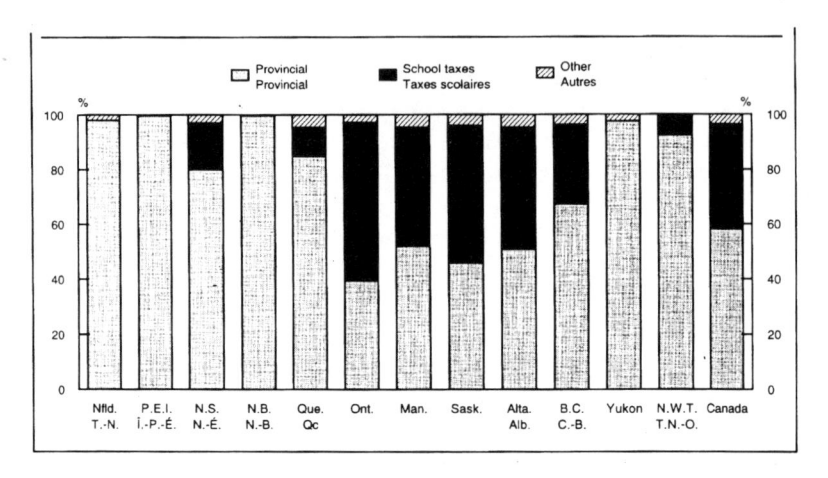

Source: Canadian Education Statistics Council *A Statistical Portrait of Elementary and Secondary Education in Canada* (Toronto: CMEC and Statistics Canada, April 1996), p. 35, graph 5.3.

In 1992, nearly 60% of school board revenues across Canada came from provincial grants; the remainder was raised through local property taxes. Local shares then ranged from almost 60 percent in Ontario to zero in Prince Edward Island and New Brunswick.[13] Current trends toward greater provincial control of school board revenues and the reduction of local board access to the property tax have significantly reduced the local share since that time. In his 1996 publication, Lawton claims that property taxes account for about one-fifth of the total revenues for elementary and secondary education.[14]

Trends in Education Finance

As we approach the year 2000, two general trends in education finance are evident in all provinces:
- Tighter control of overall expenses at the provincial level, and limits on local discretionary spending and taxing;

---

[13] *Education in Canada 1995* (Ottawa: Statistics Canada, 1996), p. 184.
[14] Stephen Lawton, *op. cit.*, p. 30.

- Significant reduction in school board budgets.[15]

As the provinces take over more responsibility for the cost of elementary and secondary education, there is a growing trend to remove school boards' access to the property tax altogether. Since 1992, Alberta and British Columbia have joined New Brunswick and Prince Edward Island in incorporating the property tax into overall provincial revenue, and Newfoundland has abolished its use for education. These five provinces now foot the entire education bill from their general revenues, which may or may not include a provincially levied property tax. Ontario proposes to cut in half its reliance on the residential property taxbase in 1998.

Sharing the Wealth

Whether provinces and territories fund all or a significant portion of the cost of elementary and secondary education, their distribution formulas are an important element of education policy. They determine how successfully and fairly a school system can meet its commitment to equity for all students. Whatever specific regulations apply to education finance, the objective is always to approach equality in both student programs and taxpayer burden. Funding regulations, which are adjusted and updated regularly, attempt to redress the inevitable inequalities created by different levels of local wealth, the special needs of individual communities, and local and regional variations in service delivery costs.

The provinces use a variety of formulas to determine an appropriate level of expenditure for each school board. These formulas are usually based on units like the number of pupils, teachers or schools within the board's jurisdiction. The units are commonly weighted according to criteria related to cost (like distance from a population centre, the seniority of teaching staff, or the special needs of students) to arrive at an appropriate grant level for each jurisdiction. Program funding, an alternative to weighted funding, bases grants on calculated average costs and estimated actual costs of program delivery.[16]

Advocates of a relatively decentralized system of education with greater local authority prefer the weighted unit approach, since it provides the greatest flexibility at the local level. Those who favour strong provincial management prefer program funding.[17] In either

---

[15] Council of Ministers of Education, Canada, *The Development of Education, op. cit.*, pp. 20-21.

[16] Stephen Lawton, *op. cit.*, p. 54.

[17] *Ibid.*, p. 56.

case, approved expenditure levels are calculated to provide an equivalent level of educational service to all students.

In provinces where the school board pays a portion of the total cost from property taxes, a second set of formulas determines how much of the approved expenditure for each board must be raised locally, and how much will be granted by the province. These formulas are generally based on a measure of local wealth, or ability to pay.

Despite efforts to distribute resources according to need and ability to pay, inequalities continue to exist. No set of formulas can possibly take account of all the factors that make some communities more difficult or costly to serve than others. In addition, some provinces allow local boards to supplement approved expenditure levels with additional levies on local residential and commercial property. As a result, wealthy communities can afford to offer enriched programs or greater program choice. Most provinces restrict such expenditures to a small percentage of the total board budget, both as a levelling measure, and to protect local taxpayers from sudden increases.

In provinces that still rely on the property tax — whether collected locally or provincially — to fund a portion of education costs, assessment policies become an integral part of education financing policies. Since owners of more valuable property pay higher taxes than owners of less valuable property, the assignment of relative value is a highly charged issue, particularly in areas with rapid growth or a volatile real estate market. The question of how frequently to re-assess is crucial, since newer properties are assessed according to current values, while older properties pay taxes based on values that are out of proportion to the current market. Adjustment factors are applied to these older properties, but they often fail to take into account changes in the real estate market. The assessment debate has been most heated in Metropolitan Toronto, where property taxes are still based on adjusted 1940s assessment values. Recently announced reforms in Ontario will include a move to a form of market value assessment.

Moves to both larger school board areas and more uniform assessment policies have helped to equalize the tax burden between the areas, and between communities within board areas.

Separate School Funding

Although provinces with two parallel school systems fund the public and separate systems equally, property taxes have worked against real equality. In Newfoundland, Alberta, Saskatchewan, Quebec and Ontario, residents have historically had the right to direct their residential, commercial and industrial taxes to the system of their choice. According to Lawton, Canada may be unique in using property taxes to support religious schools; most countries provide direct state funding of private religious schools.[18] The results have been less than equitable in Canada because in every case the public system relies on a richer tax base than the separate system.

Removing access to the tax base in favour of 100% provincial funding may address this problem. But when such changes are introduced, they raise constitutional questions about the provinces' rights to restrict local board access to property taxes. These questions hinge on the rights of separate school systems, since only they are explicitly protected in the constitution, but public school boards maintain that their rights must be presumed equivalent.

In 1994, the Alberta government replaced the local property tax with a provincial property tax, to be deposited in the Alberta School Foundation Fund. The province recognized the constitutional rights of separate school supporters, and so allowed separate school boards the option of continuing to collect their own property taxes. Public school boards challenged the provincial government, and regained the right to collect their own taxes as well. The province is appealing the court's decision.

Provinces that support separate school systems must tread carefully as they join the nation-wide trend to centralize education finance and governance at the provincial level. Again according to Lawton, "... any new arrangements for structuring or financing educational systems must be assessed against their constitutionality...".[19]

For a detailed analysis of education finance, grant formulas, and assessment issues, see Stephen Lawton's *Financing Canadian Education* (Toronto: Canadian Education Association, 1996).

---

[18] *Ibid.*, p. 103.
[19] *Ibid.*, p. 90.

Funding for Private and Independent Schools

Private schools and independent religious schools exist in all provinces. In 1991, the total expenditure for such schools amounted to $1.5 billion, more than half of which came from student fees. Some provincial funds are available to private schools in five provinces — British Columbia, Alberta, Saskatchewan, Manitoba and Quebec. Support levels are highest in Quebec, where they average 45%.[20]

The issue of funding for private schools has been particularly contentious in Ontario, where they receive no provincial support. In November 1996, the Supreme Court of Canada ruled against an appeal by the Canadian Jewish Congress and the Ontario Alliance of Christian Schools, who were seeking provincial funding for non-Catholic religious schools under the *Canadian Charter of Rights and Freedoms*. This ruling is significant, because it confirms that the *Charter* cannot be used to extend the Constitution's guarantee to fund *only* public and Roman Catholic schools. [21]

Provincial Summaries of Governance and Finance

Education finance and education governance are closely related. In keeping with the general understanding that "he who pays the piper calls the tune," the shifting of responsibilities and the shifting of financial burden go hand in hand. In virtually every province, the 1990s have been characterized by those shifts, which are mentioned in the following summary. However, in the current climate of change in education, no summary of the state of either governance or finance is likely to remain current for long.[22]

Newfoundland and Labrador

Newfoundland and Labrador's former 27 denominational school boards have been reduced to ten uni- or inter-denominational boards

---

[20] Council of Ministers of Education, Canada, *The Development of Education, op. cit.*, p. 25.

[21] Ontario Public School Boards' Association, *Fast Reports: Weekly Information for Decision-makers in Education*, vol. 8, no. 37 (22 November 1996).

[22] Material from the following section has been compiled from: CMEC, *op. cit.*, pp 20-21; *Who's Running our Schools? Education Governance in the 90's. Provincial/Territorial Summaries* (Ottawa: CSBA, 1995); *CEA Newsletter*, December 1996, pp. 1-3.

with 18 members each. This change required an amendment to Newfoundland's 1949 union with Canada, which was approved by the Canadian House of Commons and Senate in 1996.

In Newfoundland and Labrador, property taxes and poll taxes for education were abolished in 1992-93. Education is now funded 100% provincially. Teachers' salaries and benefits are paid directly by the province. The province provides no funding for private schools.

Prince Edward Island

In 1994, Prince Edward Island's five school boards were merged into three (two anglophone, one francophone). Education is funded 100% provincially. Private schools are not funded.

Nova Scotia

Nova Scotia's 22 school boards were regrouped into seven in 1996, and they work in consultation with school advisory councils. The province provides about 80% of education funding; the balance is raised from municipal taxes, approved by the municipality. The school boards have no powers of taxation. Nova Scotia provides no support for private schools.

New Brunswick

New Brunswick dissolved all school boards in March, 1996, and the Minister of Education assumed all their rights, responsibilities and obligations. School and district parent councils will advise at the school level, and two provincial boards of education (one anglophone, one francophone) have been established to advise the minister. In New Brunswick, education is funded 100% by the province, with some user fee provisions. Teacher salaries are determined provincially. There is no funding for private schools.

Quebec

Plans to reduce the number of boards in Quebec from 158 to 70 and to re-organize the system along linguistic lines are under way. The province provides 82.8% of education funding. Local taxes account for 10.6%, and other sources (e.g. user fees) for the remaining 6.6%. Extra expenditures are not eligible for grants, and can only exceed a specified level by referendum. At present, an average of 55.9% of private school costs are funded by the province; this policy is under review.

Ontario

Ontario's government has cut the number of school boards in half, from 129 to 72 (plus 31 small, isolate school authorities). New "district" school boards will have fewer trustees and lose the right to raise their own revenue from the local tax base. Local taxes have paid more than half of Ontario's education costs; under the new system, the province will set residential and business property tax levels, and reduce the local share of education funding by about one-third. Private schools receive no financial assistance from the government.

Manitoba

The Manitoba School Divisions/Districts Boundaries Review Commission recommended the number of school boards be reduced from 57 to 21. However, the government is leaving the amalgamation decision to local boards. Manitoba provides approximately 70% of the cost of education provincially; school divisions raise the balance through local property taxes. Of the provincial share, about 75% is provided through the consolidated revenues, and 25% from a provincial levy on property assessment. Private schools that meet provincial criteria receive partial funding.

Saskatchewan

Saskatchewan is requiring school boards to participate in restructuring discussions, but any restructuring will be locally initiated and determined. Saskatchewan provides 44% provincial funding, with the remainder supported by local taxes on residential and non-residential property. Only two categories of independent schools are funded: "historical high schools" and alternative schools.

Alberta

Alberta reduced the number of its school boards to 64 in 1997. At the same time, the province took control of most property taxes, and directed them to the Alberta School Foundation Fund. School boards can levy an additional 3% locally. Private schools receive 35% funding.

British Columbia

British Columbia has amalgamated 31 of its school boards into 15 larger units, and leaving 44 boards unchanged. The province uses a block resource cost funding model, based on the cost of providing for specific needs. Local taxes are collected by municipalities and forwarded to the province. Discretionary residential taxes must be approved by referendum. Three groups of private schools receive different percentages of partial funding.

Yukon

The Yukon Department of education operates the school system with one school committee and school councils. Yukon established its first school board, a francophone board in Whitehorse, in 1996. The territorial government funds all education costs. Private schools do not receive funding.

Northwest Territories

The Northwest Territories operates eight divisional school boards and two school districts (in Yellowknife). The districts raise local taxes to pay for approximately 25% of the K-9 program. All other costs are funded by the territorial government. There are no private schools.

Canada's Schools: A Profile

Canada's elementary and secondary schools are as diverse as the nation itself. From remote arctic communities, to sprawling Western Canadian school districts, to densely populated cities, Canadian children attend school almost without exception. Their schools reflect the values and priorities of their communities, but they also expose young Canadians from vastly different backgrounds to the richness of their national heritage, and to the challenges and opportunities of the twenty-first century. In this profile of elementary and secondary education in Canada, it is important to remember that schools are more than statistics and regulations. They are the incubators of new talents and new ideas that will shape the future of Canada.

The School Population

More than five million students attend Canada's 16,000 elementary and secondary schools. They range in age from four to adult; they attend inner-city schools with 2,000 students and isolated schools with 20; they study in two official languages and share many cultures of origin. Some students walk a few minutes to school; some are bused long distances; and some live in such remote communities that they must move to larger cities to complete their high school education.

Compulsory schooling begins at age six in Newfoundland, Nova Scotia, Quebec, Ontario, Alberta, British Columbia and the Northwest Territories, and at age seven in Prince Edward Island, New Brunswick, Manitoba, Saskatchewan and the Yukon. The minimum school leaving age is 16 across the country.

In any nation with compulsory schooling, school enrolment statistics mirror demographic statistics. Canada's school population reached a peak of 5.8 million in 1970-71.[23] As the post-war baby boom generation passed through the school system, enrolments began to drop — by more than half a million between 1971 and 1991. They rebounded somewhat during the late 1980s and 1990s, when the children of the baby-boomers reached school age. These increases were supplemented by an expansion of pre-school and adult education programs. Levels are expected to stabilize between 1996 and 2001, and fall again after the turn of the century, in keeping with the aging of the general population.[24]

The birth rate pattern is the major determinant of school enrolment, but not the only one. Immigration and emigration, adult education, part-time attendance in the higher grades, and optional programs for four- and five-year-olds also have an impact, as do social and economic trends. For example, children with two working parents are more likely to attend pre-schools, and students are more likely to stay in school when outside employment is hard to find.

Graduation Rates

Since the 1960s a secondary school diploma has become a minimum educational requirement for most jobs in Canada. Unemployment rates for those without a secondary school diploma are 12.8%, compared to 8.5% for those with a diploma, and 6.5% for those with a post-secondary diploma or degree.[25]

In the general population, level of education is closely correlated to age. Among Canadians age 65 and over, fewer than 40% have graduated from high school; almost 80% of those between 20 and 24 have a high school diploma.[26] In recent decades, all provinces have concentrated on improving high school graduation rates, which have continued to rise in the 1980s and 1990s — from 66% in 1988-89 to 73% in 1992-93. They range from a low of 25% in the Northwest Territories

---

[23] Council of Ministers of Education, Canada, *The Development ..., op. cit.*, p. 16.
[24] Canadian Education Statistics Council, *A Statistical Portrait, op. cit.*, p. 6.
[25] *Education Quarterly Review, op. cit.*, p. 54.
[26] Canadian Education Statistics Council, *A Statistical Portrait, op. cit.*, p. 22.

to a high of 83% in New Brunswick, with most provinces falling near the average.

These figures can be misleading. They do not include adults who return to school, change jurisdictions during high school, or obtain their high school equivalency outside the high school system. If they did, graduation rates would be higher for all jurisdictions, but particularly for Quebec, where adult education is prevalent.[27] A 1993 Statistics Canada report, *Leaving School*, puts the national drop-out rate at 18%, if students returning to school and transferring to other jurisdictions are taken into account.[28] This figure is consistent with the 80% of young adults who report that they have completed secondary school.

Participation rates during the non-compulsory years are one way of measuring the public school system's relevance to students. At 15 and 16, virtually all young people are still in school. After they pass the age of compulsory schooling, their participation rate begins to decrease, to about 75% at age 17, 40% at 18, and 10% at 19. It should be noted that by age 17, Quebec students have entered the college system (cégeps), and by ages 18 and 19 most students elsewhere in Canada have graduated from secondary school.[29]

Participation Rates by Age, by Province and Territory, Canada, 1992 -93

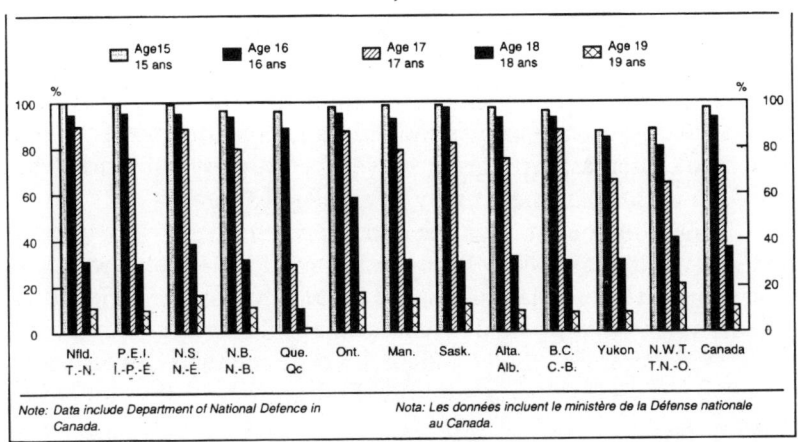

Source: Canadian Education Statistics Council, *A Statistical Portrait of Elementary and Secondary Education in Canada* (Toronto: CMEC and Statistics Canada, April 1996), p. 15, graph 2.3.

---

[27] *Ibid.*, p. 20.
[28] Council of Ministers of Education, Canada, *The Development...*, *op. cit.*, p. 30.
[29] Canadian Education Statistics Council, *A Statistical Portrait*, *op. cit.*, p. 14.

Pre-school Programs

Studies of school success invariably emphasize the importance of early childhood learning experiences. School attendance is not mandatory in any province until grade 1 (usually age 6), but all provinces except Prince Edward Island offer kindergarten programs for 5-year-olds. Although not compulsory, kindergarten has become an integral part of provincial public education systems, with participation rates in most provinces above 90%. A number of provinces also offer a pre-kindergarten (or junior kindergarten) program for 4-year-olds. Ontario is the only province where most 4-year-olds were enrolled in a school program in 1992-93.[30] Recently the Ontario government made junior kindergarten optional rather than mandatory, so this level of participation is not likely to continue.

Kindergarten programs are designed to prepare students for the more formal learning environment of grade 1. They use a play-based program to enhance children's social, emotional, physical and intellectual development. Kindergarten is usually a half-day program, but a number of school boards have moved to full days on alternate days as a cost-saving measure. Some school boards in Manitoba, Ontario and Quebec combine 4- and 5-year-olds in a two-year pre-school program.

Alberta has a co-ordinated system of local and provincial programs called Early Childhood Services, which began in 1974. About 98% of Alberta children aged four-and-a-half attend programs run by school boards, private schools and private ECS centres. Most children enter the kindergarten program one year before entry into grade 1, but children with special needs may be enrolled earlier.

Eligibility for kindergarten entry varies from province to province. Newfoundland, New Brunswick, Ontario, Manitoba, Saskatchewan, British Columbia, Yukon, and the Northwest Territories admit children who have turned five years of age by December 31 (or four for junior kindergarten, where available). Nova Scotia and Quebec use an October 1 cut-off; Alberta requires children to be five years old by September 1.[31]

---

[30] *Ibid.*

[31] Austin J. Harte, *Improving School Attendance: Responsibility and Challenge* (Toronto: Canadian Education Association, 1994), p 31.

School Organization

Canadian school systems are organized into two major divisions: elementary, which usually includes children from kindergarten through grade 6 or 8; and secondary, which prepares them for graduation. The point of transition from elementary to secondary school varies from province to province, as do the age-groupings within elementary schools. The two most common organizational structures are: K - 8 (elementary), followed by 9 - 12 (secondary); and K - 6 (elementary), followed by 7 - 9 (junior high school or middle school) and 10 - 12 (secondary).

Ontario is the only province that provides for an optional fifth year of secondary school to prepare for university. Recently introduced reforms in that province will bring it into line with the other provinces by creating a four-year secondary school program, beginning with the cohort entering grade 9 in 1999.

The School Day and School Year

The school year varies from 180 to 200 instructional days, typically beginning in late August or early September and ending in late June. (In the far north of Yukon and Northwest Territories, where days are longer in June, school begins mid-August and closes the first week in June.) All schools observe national and provincial statutory holidays. In addition to summer vacation, Canadian elementary and secondary students enjoy two major holidays: seven to ten days at Christmas (at least from December 23 to January 2), and a spring break, usually a week in March or April. A few school boards have experimented with year-round schooling, in which students have several shorter breaks instead of the two-month summer holiday.

The length of the school day can vary from province to province, and provincial legislation may give school boards some flexibility in setting the hours of their school day. School typically begins between 8:30 and 9:00 a.m. and ends between 3:00 and 4:00 p.m., with an average of five hours of instruction (plus lunch and recess) for elementary students, and five-and-a-half hours for secondary school students.

Textbooks and Learning Materials

In most provinces, school boards provide textbooks free of charge for both elementary and secondary school students, who return their books at the end of the course or school year.

Principals and teachers choose from a list of textbooks approved by their department or ministry of education. Preference is given to materials written by Canadians and published in Canada. Schools may use unlisted texts and supplementary materials only after obtaining permission from the Minister of Education.

School boards in all provinces except Ontario and Quebec purchase textbooks through a central office, called the school book bureau or curriculum resources division. It operates as an adjunct to the department of education, and purchases bulk shipments of authorized texts for distribution to the schools.

Elementary Schools

Children come to elementary school from a play-based preschool or home environment. By the time they leave, six or eight years later, they are entering adolescence. As a rule, elementary schools gradually move children from a less structured, play-based learning environment to one that is more structured and formal, in preparation for secondary school.

Elementary schools concentrate on the basic skills of reading, writing and mathematics, plus science, social studies, physical and health education, music and art. In most Canadian schools, second language instruction (English or French) is also introduced at the elementary level. In denominational schools, religious instruction is a part of the curriculum.

School Organization

The average Canadian elementary school accommodates 250 students, although almost one-fifth have more than 400. Most assign a classroom teacher to a class of 20 to 30 students in a single grade, or in two consecutive grades. Primary classes (kindergarten through grade 3 or 4) are kept as small as possible — by regulation in some provinces. Other teachers may come into the classroom to teach specialized subjects like music, art, physical education, or a second language, but the classroom teacher is responsible for meeting the basic curriculum objectives for the class over the course of a school year.

A fluctuating student population, combined with a need to use resources efficiently, has led to a growing number of split-grade classrooms at the elementary level. These are classes which combine two (occasionally three) consecutive grades, taught by one teacher. A 1991 study by the Canadian Education Association found that one of seven classrooms in Canada is multi-grade, that approximately one of every five elementary students is enrolled in a multi-grade classroom, and that children in split-grade classrooms do as well as their counterparts in single-grade classrooms.

Teaching Methods and Evaluation

Some schools organize learning strictly according to discrete subject areas and time on task; others integrate a number of subject areas into a flexible schedule.

Since the 1970s, Canadian educators have been debating the relative merits of progressive (or child-centred) education and more traditional, teacher-directed methods. The predominant focus in Canada has been on the child-centred approach, but recent changes in many provinces have re-focused the elementary classroom on core subjects, clear benchmarks, and measurable outcomes. Some have introduced province-wide student testing in specific subjects and at certain grade levels.

Even where such tests exist, they are not used alone to measure student success. Classroom teachers at the elementary level evaluate their students continuously. Those who are not achieving at expected levels receive remedial assistance, either within the classroom or in the school's resource centre.

Report cards are issued several times each year to give parents an indication of their student's progress. Some provinces and some school boards use anecdotal report cards, others use letter grades or percentages. Generally, reporting becomes more objective as children move into higher grades, and some provinces are moving toward less subjective reporting, even in the lower grades, in an attempt to improve accountability to parents and students.

Most Canadian elementary schools avoid holding children back to repeat a grade. They prefer to move the children from grade to grade with their age group, providing help when necessary, and "repeating" only as a last resort.

Secondary Schools

The goal of the secondary school (or high school) system is to prepare students for post-secondary studies or employment. Most Canadian secondary schools combine academic and vocational programs under one roof; a few jurisdictions still maintain separate vocational high schools which specialize in specific job and trade-related programs, and some offer short programs preparing students for specific trades.

School Organization
Secondary schools tend to be larger than elementary schools, averaging about 600 students, with more than half at 400 or more. They are usually organized by subject area; students move from classroom to classroom, where teachers provide courses in their subject. In some schools, particularly in the early years of secondary school, classes of students move as a group from class to class. By the time they reach their senior years, most students have individualized timetables.

Many secondary schools operate on a two-semester system, particularly at the senior grades.

The Credit System
In order to meet diploma requirements, secondary students in every province must complete a combination of compulsory and elective subjects required by the provincial Ministry or Department of Education. These are offered as individual credits, which are awarded on a course-by-course basis, allowing students some flexibility in planning their secondary program. The first years of secondary school are usually devoted to compulsory credits, which may be available at varying degrees of difficulty. By the later years, students may specialize by choosing electives which support their post-graduation choices: university, college or the workplace.

Progress through secondary school is measured by credits achieved rather than by years completed. At the secondary level, students are given letter grades or percentages for each course. Course grades are based on a combination of class assignments, tests and exams. Usually the school issues one or two interim report cards before the end of the course.

Qualifications for Graduation

Compulsory subjects vary from province to province. They include first-language studies (English or French), mathematics, sciences, arts, social studies, physical education, and second-language instruction. Most provinces also offer health, personal and social skills training, home economics, industrial training, computer studies and technology.[32]

A number of provinces have been revising their secondary school graduation requirements to reflect the growing shift toward tighter standards and more uniform programs. The move away from student-centred learning toward a more traditional approach has resulted in fewer electives in some provinces, and some provinces are returning to provincially set examinations as a requirement for graduation.

Provincial Summary of Diploma Requirements

In the following summary of diploma requirements for each province and territory, it should be noted that the definition of a "credit" varies from province to province, accounting for the great variation in credit requirements. In Alberta, for example, a credit represents 25 hours of instruction, in Newfoundland, 55-60 hours, and in Ontario, Manitoba and Prince Edward Island, 110 hours of instruction.

In British Columbia, a student must earn 52 credits in grades 11 and 12 in order to graduate. Most courses are four credits each. Of the 52 credits, 28 must be earned in foundations studies, 10 must be provincially approved electives, and 14 can be other electives such as locally developed courses. Provincial examinations are required in English, communications, or *français langue* (for those studying in French), as well as for many elective grade 12 courses. The provincial exam accounts for 40% of the student's final mark.

The Yukon follows British Columbia's basic program, graduation requirements and examination system.

To obtain an Alberta High School Diploma, students must earn a minimum of 100 credits in grades 10 through 12, including required courses in English, social studies, science, mathematics, physical

---

[32] Council of Ministers of Education, Canada, *The Development of Education, op. cit.*, p. 27.

education, and career and life management. Provincial diploma examinations are required in grade 12 academic courses. An Alberta high school credit represents the knowledge, skills and attitudes that most students can achieve with about 25 hours of instruction. Students must write a minimum of two provincial diploma examinations (English and social studies) to obtain a diploma.

The Northwest Territories uses Alberta's provincial diploma exams for core grade 12 subjects, and much of its curriculum is similar to Alberta's. For a diploma, students need 100 credits earned in grade 10 through grade 12. In addition to English, social studies, mathematics, and science, compulsory subjects include northern studies, fine arts, career and life management, and community service.

In Saskatchewan, students must acquire 24 credits during secondary school, five of which must be at the grade 12 level. Grade 11 and 12 credits must include English, social studies, science, social science and math. Departmental examinations are required for grade 12 academic subjects if the teacher is not accredited in that subject.

Manitoba offers diplomas in both English and French. Students need to complete 28 credits in grades 9 through 12. Fourteen credits (18 credits for a diploma in French) are compulsory in language arts, mathematics, science, social studies, and physical education/health. A compulsory complementary social studies course is also required at the grade 11 level until further notice. Province-wide examinations are given in designated subjects and provide a proportion of the students' final marks. A student may earn one credit by successfully completing a course designed for a minimum of 110 hours of instruction. Half-credits may be earned in like manner (55 hours).

Ontario requires 30 credits for graduation, of which 16 are compulsory. Each credit represents 110 hours of instruction. Students proceeding to university are required to complete six Ontario Academic Courses (OACs), which may be included in the 30, or completed in addition to the 30. The province is reviewing the structure of secondary school in order to put in place a new four-year system.

In Quebec, secondary school lasts five years and follows six years of primary school. Required courses throughout secondary school include language arts (French or English), a second language (English or French), mathematics, physical education, and confessional moral and religious education, or moral education. To obtain a secondary school diploma, students must accumulate 54 credits, of which 20 must be taken in the final year. They must pass school or ministry examinations after the fourth and fifth years. Students proceeding to post-secondary programs move from secondary school to one of Quebec's *collèges d'enseignement général et professionnel (cégeps)*, which also offer technical training courses.

New Brunswick requires anglophone students to obtain 20 credits, including 15 compulsory courses: seven in language and mathematics, three in science and technology, two in social sciences, two in personal development, and one additional course from any of the above clusters. Students normally take eight courses for each of the three years of high school. Plans are under way to remove the credit system from grade 10, and to require students to pass 14 of 16 credits in grades 11 and 12, including two mathematics, two English, one science, one social studies, and one fine arts or life role development. Students in francophone schools must obtain a minimum of 26 credits including 23 compulsory courses over their four years of high school: six in *français*, five in *mathématiques*, three in science (*biologie, chimie, physique*), three in social studies (*sciences sociales, histoire, géographie*), two in *anglais langue seconde*, one in *éducation artistique*, one in *éducation physique*, one in *formation personnelle et sociale*, one in *technologie*, and one of either *développement humain, institutions politiques, économiques et juridiques, entrepreneurial* or *éducation artistique*. The present requirements will be reviewed in light of *L'École secondaire renouvelée*. Each sector sets its own provincial examinations.

In Nova Scotia, students must obtain 18 credits for graduation, including three language arts, one fine arts, one social studies, one global studies, two mathematics, two science, two additional credits from technology, mathematics, or science, and two half-credits in physically active lifestyles and career and life management.

Prince Edward Island requires students to complete 18 110-hour credits, including four language, two mathematics, two science, and two social studies. These requirements are under review, which may result in a move to a 20-credit graduation requirement.

Newfoundland and Labrador requires students to attain 36 credits, representing 55-60 hours of instruction each. At least 20 credits must be obtained above Level I, and at least nine must be obtained at Level III or IV. In the anglophone system, students are required to obtain credits in three English language, four English literature, four mathematics, four science, two Canada studies, two world studies, two economic education, plus four credits in any other subject area and 11 in any subject area. Requirements in the French First Language Program are identical, except the English language and literature requirements are replaced by six credits in français and four credits in either anglais (second language) or English language/literature.

All provinces and territories, except Quebec, offer General Education Development (GED) testing to give adults an opportunity to earn high school equivalency on the strength of their life and work experiences. The tests cover writing skills, social studies, science, reading skills, and mathematics. They emphasize skills of comprehension, critical evaluation and clear thinking rather than detailed content. Quebec has developed comparable tests with the same objectives.

Correspondence education and distance learning is also available across the country, for students who are unable to obtain their required credits in a secondary school setting.

Language Instruction

Bilingualism is a defining characteristic of Canada and language policies are a defining characteristic of its school systems. The country's English-speaking majority (71%) is largely found outside Quebec. Within Quebec, 85% of the population speaks French as a first language. New Brunswick has the second-highest French-speaking population (32%), and is the only officially bilingual province. [33]

The federal government's Official Languages in Education Program was introduced following the 1969 recognition of French and English as Canada's two official languages. Its objectives were twofold: to ensure that francophones outside Quebec, and anglophones in Quebec, had access to school programs in their own language; and to provide opportunities for unilingual Canadians to learn their other official language.

The *Constitution Act* of 1982 and the *Charter of Rights and Freedoms* cemented these objectives by providing formal guarantees of minority language rights for elementary and secondary education. The charter guarantees that children will receive instruction in the minority language of their province if it is their mother tongue (first language learned and spoken in the home); if it is the language in which their parents were educated; or if it is the language in which other children in the family are being or have been educated. These criteria apply in all provinces and territories except Quebec, where the criterion of mother tongue does not apply. They are subject to a "where numbers warrant" clause, which allows the provinces to set a minimum number of eligible students, without which school boards are exempt from the

---

[33] Canadian Education Statistics Council, *A Statistical Portrait, op. cit.*, p. 14.

requirement to establish and maintain second language school programs.

In 1984, Ontario passed legislation which in effect negated the "where numbers warrant" provision by requiring school boards in that province to provide French-language education to francophone students who meet the constitutional criteria, regardless of number.

Under bilateral agreements, the federal government provides financial assistance to the provinces and territories for the additional costs they incur in developing and maintaining language services. In 1992-93, it transferred $296.5 million to the provinces through the Official Languages Program.[34]

Three levels of language instruction are commonly available in Canadian schools:

Minority language programs are designed to ensure that all francophone and anglophone children in Canada have access to schooling in their first language. These programs are delivered in French-language schools for francophone children and English-language schools for anglophone children. They are the only language programs that are subject to constitutional guarantees.

French immersion programs, which flourish in urban areas across the country, are designed to teach French as a second language. They usually begin in the early grades. English-speaking children are immersed in French programs beginning in kindergarten, and receive all of their early school program in French. In later grades, when they have established fluency in French, English is introduced as a language of instruction for part of the school day. By secondary school, immersion students usually take a combination of English and French classes when the option is available. Some school boards also offer late entry immersion programs, which begin in late elementary or early secondary grades.

French immersion programs are available in all provinces and territories, but not in all communities. They tend to be concentrated in urban areas, where the demand justifies the cost. In 1992-93, 7% of non-francophone students outside Quebec, and 25% in Quebec, were enrolled in French immersion programs.

Regular second language programs provide students with instruction in the second official language as a core subject. In many provinces, French is compulsory after grade 4 or 5, but it is often offered earlier. In Quebec, English is a compulsory subject from grade 4 through graduation.

---

[34] *Canada Year Book, 1997* (Ottawa: Statistics Canada, 1997), p. 136.

Language Programs for Immigrant Students

Immigration is a major contributor to Canada's population growth, and an area of national policy that touches the classroom directly. Of the approximately 200,000 immigrants who enter the country each year, nearly one-quarter are of school age. Although these numbers do not represent a large percentage of the Canadian school population, they have a large impact in some areas. In major urban areas — particularly Toronto, Montreal and Vancouver — immigrant children form a significant proportion of the elementary and secondary school population. In 1992, more than half of Canada's 45,000 immigrant children and youth settled in Ontario and nearly a quarter in Quebec. British Columbia followed with 13.4%, and Alberta with 6.6%. In a recent trend, school-age immigration rates have been increasing in Quebec while declining slightly elsewhere in Canada.[35]

Approximately two-thirds of all school-age immigrants speak neither English nor French. An influx of students from different cultural backgrounds has led many school boards to develop or expand programs in English or French as a second language, and to introduce orientation and counselling programs for new immigrant students. In keeping with its language and cultural protection policies, Quebec legislation requires all children in that province, whose mother tongue is neither French nor English, to attend French schools.

Some provinces have introduced heritage language courses in response to immigrant families who want their children to identify with their culture of origin, as well as with Canada. Heritage language usually refers to all modern languages other than English or French; some jurisdictions include aboriginal languages. Although these programs are controversial, they are now available in six provinces: Quebec, Ontario, Manitoba, Saskatchewan, Alberta and British Columbia. Ontario requires school boards to provide heritage language programs when a single language is requested by the parents of more than 25 students. In all other provinces the program is left to the discretion of local school boards.

Heritage language programs range from a few classes with a handful of students, to classes in 72 Quebec schools, to Ontario's 4,000 classes, with 96,000 students learning more than 60 different languages. With few exceptions, heritage languages are offered only in the elementary grades. Some boards integrate them into the school day; others use a bilingual format; still others offer classes after school,

---

[35] Canadian Education Statistics Council, *Education Indicators, op. cit.*, p. 32.

in the evenings, or on weekends. The time allotment is generally from 100 to 150 minutes per week.

Education for Native Children

The federal government, through the Department of Indian and Northern Affairs, has direct responsibility for the education of status Indians normally resident on Reserves and Inuit. This special relationship is the result of long-standing treaty obligations between the Government of Canada and the First Nations. The history of education of the Native peoples of Canada is sadly lacking in respect for their Native languages, cultures, and world-views. In fact, those languages and cultures were suppressed in the name of assimilation as a generation of Native children was sent off to residential schools to learn the English or French language and Canadian culture. More than 60 of these schools were still in operation as recently as the 1960s.[36] Most have since been closed; only six or seven are still in operation.

Native communities have been working to improve the quality and relevance of educational programs for their children. At the elementary and secondary level, they have gained local control of many of their own schools, emphasized the teaching of Native languages, introduced curriculum materials developed for and by Native people, encouraged community involvement in the education of young people, and introduced programs to attract Natives to the teaching profession.

Native people make up approximately 3% of Canada's population. Some 74,000 Canadians report Cree as their mother tongue, and 24,000 Inuktituk. In the Northwest Territories, almost 40% of households speak a Native language.[37] The general term "Native" is usually inclusive, referring to status and non-status Indians, Inuit and Métis.

Status Indians are those registered with one of the country's 608 Indian bands. Of Canada's more than half million status Indians, 60% live on Reserves. Ontario is the single province with the largest population of status Indians, approximately 135,000, but the greatest concentration lives in the western and prairie provinces (60%).[38]

---

[36] "Indian Residential Schools," Information Sheet (April 1993. http://www.inac.gc.ca/pubs/information/info46.html).

[37] Council of Ministers of Education, Canada, *The Development of Education, op. cit.*, p. 9.

[38] "Facts from Stats: Basic Departmental Data" (Issue No. 11), March-April 1996. (www.inac.gc.ca/stats/ facts/stats.html)

Non-status Indians are those with aboriginal ancestry who are not registered with a band, and are not eligible to live on Reserves.

The Canadian Inuit (Eskimo) population of approximately 30,000 lives primarily in the Northwest Territories, northern Quebec, Labrador, and in settlements throughout the Arctic islands.[39]

Métis are of mixed French and Indian extraction. Canada's 75,000 Métis are concentrated in Manitoba, Saskatchewan and Alberta.[40]

Canada's Native population is markedly younger than the population as a whole. In 1994, more than 50% of Registered Indians were under 25 years of age, compared to 34% of the general population.[41] As a result, Native children make up a larger proportion of the school-age and young adult population than general population statistics would indicate.

The federal government meets its responsibility for Native education in one of two ways.

Federal schools. Only nine schools are operated directly by the Department of Indian and Northern Affairs; the rest are run by Indian bands themselves, with the assistance of federal funding. The number of band-operated schools has more than doubled from 203 in 1985 to 429 in 1996. The percentage of Indian children in band-operated elementary and secondary schools rose from 20% in 1985 to 54% in 1995.[42] The educational programs in federal and band-operated schools are similar to those offered by local school boards, with an additional emphasis on Native culture and languages.

In some remote Native communities, on-Reserve schooling is only available through the elementary or early secondary grades. Students who wish to proceed to secondary school must either make arrangements to board in larger towns or cities, or complete their education by means of correspondence or distance education.

Federal Support to Public Schools. All status Indian students living off Reserve, and many living on Reserve, attend their province's public schools. The federal government transfers funds to the provincial government or school board to cover the costs of these students. Schools with significant numbers of Native students are permitted to revise their curriculum to include Native culture and languages, frequently taught by Native education specialists.

---

[39] *Canada Year Book 1997, op. cit.,* p. 88.
[40] *Ibid.*
[41] "Facts from Stats: Statistics on Registered Indians " (Issue No. 12), May 1996. (www.inac.gc.ca/stats/facts/ bdd95.html).
[42] *Ibid.*

Métis and non-status Indian students attend local public elementary and secondary schools. They have no special status vis-à-vis the federal government, but can often take advantage of public school programs designed to benefit Native students.

It is widely recognized that Native students are more motivated to succeed in school when they are exposed to Native teachers as role models. In 1968, the Northwest Territories broke new ground in North America when it began preparing Native people for teaching careers by adapting its teacher education program to reflect Native culture. In 1981, this approach was extended to include a field-based option that allows teachers to be trained without spending long periods of time away from home. In 1990, Yukon College, in conjunction with the University of Regina, began a Native teacher education program for students with no post-secondary background. In this home-based program, students alternate between two weeks in class and two weeks in a school in their own community. In the same year, Arctic College in the Northwest Territories began using a home-based approach in its community teacher education project for aboriginal language groups in the West Arctic.

School boards across the country have introduced programs to improve the success rates of Native students. They usually include Native language programs, either as part of the regular school day or in after school classes. The Toronto Board of Education has designated one school specifically for Native children, where Native themes are integrated into all subjects, and Ojibwa is taught from 20 to 40 minutes a day. In British Columbia, the First Nations Congress Education Secretariat is an official advisory body to the Ministry of Education. In 1989, Alberta launched a Native education policy to promote partnerships among Native people, school boards and the department of education.

In 1996, the federal government introduced a First Nations School Co-op Education Program to help First Nations schools establish or expand their co-operative education programs. The program is designed to provide opportunities for high school students to combine school-based learning with workplace experience.

There is evidence that the efforts of Native communities, governments and school boards are paying off. In 1985, only 31% of Indian children remained in school until grade 12. By 1995, that percentage had more than doubled to 73% — close to the national average.[43]

---

[43] *Ibid.*

Special Education

All provinces and territories have taken steps, either in policy directives or in legislation, to ensure that special education is available to students who need it. The exceptionalities generally recognized as eligible for special education services include: cognitive impairment, emotional impairment, learning disabilities, physical disabilities, communications disorders, sensory impairments (vision, hearing), multiple disabilities, and other health-related impairments. Gifted students are also considered exceptional, and are eligible for special programs in some provinces.[44]

The trend throughout Canada is to move exceptional children out of segregated classrooms and schools, and to integrate them with children of their own age. However, individual circumstances frequently complicate the decision about appropriate placement. On the one hand, parents sometimes insist on integration even when the school board cannot accommodate the child in an integrated setting. On the other hand, some parents feel that a separate class would serve their child best when such a class in unavailable or unaffordable. Recently the Supreme Court of Canada ruled that an Ontario school board acted within its rights when it chose to override the wishes of parents to place their severely disabled child in a regular classroom. This ruling confirms that school boards have the final responsibility for placement, after taking into consideration the best interests of both the individual child and the classes affected.

Special educators make a distinction between integration and "mainstreaming," which is the term used when special students are expected to cope without extra assistance in a regular classroom. In theory, integration sets realistic expectations and provides special students with the supports they need to learn in a classroom of their peers.

In practice, teachers often feel unprepared to cope with the requirements of special students in an integrated classroom. Many classroom teachers lack specific training in special education, and special education students often require a disproportionate amount of a teacher's time. As a result, the move toward integration has been accompanied by an increase in teaching assistants, assigned either to the whole classroom or to individual students with special needs.

Some students clearly benefit from intensive instruction in a

---

[44] Council of Ministers of Education, Canada, *The Development of Education, op. cit.*, p. 32.

separate environment which is beyond the ability of most local school systems to provide. More than 2,000 Canadian children are enrolled in 19 provincially-operated schools for the sight or hearing impaired, including two in Nova Scotia which are operated jointly under the Atlantic Provinces Special Education Authority. Some provinces also operate schools for the trainable retarded, for children with severe learning disabilities, and for those in care, under treatment and in correctional facilities.

Education or Social Service?

Canadian educators have a hard time drawing the line between education and social service. Children who are hungry, frightened, or emotionally troubled cannot learn. During the 1970s and 1980s, many school boards began introducing programs to meet the needs of these students; they began free breakfast and lunch programs, hired social workers, provided in-school counselling. While boards continued to remind provincial governments that these services were beyond their educational mandate, they also continued to fill the gaps left by provincial and local social service agencies.

During the fiscally tight 1990s, boards have had to concentrate scarce resources on core educational programs. As a result, many of these school-based social services are being abandoned, or picked up by other community agencies.

Private Schools

Private schools — known as independent schools in most provinces outside Quebec — complement the public and separate school systems in every province. Although independent from the two public school systems, they must provide programs of study that meet provincial standards in order to grant graduation diplomas. They are, however, free to offer alternatives that reflect the philosophy and values of the communities they serve.

About half of all independent schools have a religious affiliation. Others adhere to particular teaching methods or styles (e.g., Montessori schools, Waldorf schools), focus on particular curriculum areas (science, performing arts, sports), stress academic excellence, or meet the needs of students with special talents or special needs. Most are smaller than public schools (almost 75% have fewer than 200 students).[45]

---

[45] *Ibid.*, p. 32.

Since 1971, there has been a gradual increase in private school enrolment, from 2.5% to approximately 5% of total enrolment. The Canadian Teachers' Federation estimates that private school enrolment increased 4.2% between 1994 and 1996, while public school enrolment grew by just 1.8%. Quebec private school attendance rate is the highest in the country, at 9.2% of the total. Other provinces showing marked increases are British Columbia, Alberta and Nova Scotia.[46]

Although in some provinces independent schools receive limited provincial funding, virtually all charge student fees to cover costs. Most have bursary or tuition relief programs to subsidize the cost of children whose parents cannot afford full fees.

Some provinces are forestalling the growth of private schools by allowing boards to incorporate alternative schools within their own systems. In Alberta and Saskatchewan, private schools may become alternative or associate schools with publicly funded school boards. Alberta is the only province to sanction and fund charter schools, which it defines as public schools with a special mandate to improve student learning through innovations.[47] These schools operate independently of local school boards, but receive provincial funding. They may not charge tuition fees, or be affiliated with a religious faith (except in the case of a charter approved by a separate school board). Charter school students must write provincial achievement tests and high school diploma exams, and teachers at charter schools must be certified.

Special Subject Schools

Not all parents need to turn to private schools for a specialized elementary or secondary program for their children. In urban areas, school boards often maintain schools with a special focus, like music, drama, science, technology, or traditional academic subjects. Students gain admission to these specialized schools through a board-approved screening process. Because they are part of the public (or separate) school system, these specialized schools adhere to all provincial requirements and standards, while providing extra emphasis on areas of special interest.

---

[46] *Ibid.*, p. 33.
[47] Canadian School Boards Association, *Who's Running Our Schools? Provincial/Territorial Summaries, op. cit.*, p. 56.

Home Schooling

Although school attendance is compulsory in Canada, every province permits home-schooling for parents who wish to take personal responsibility for educating their children. Parents are required to register their children and to follow guidelines and policies set by the province. Local school board officials typically monitor the progress of home-schooled children in their jurisdiction. Some provinces provide funds to the parents to help defray the costs of learning at home and to the local school board to help compensate for the costs of registering and monitoring student progress.

Between 20,000 and 25,000 Canadian students take some or all of their elementary and secondary education at home. In Alberta, 6,000 children were home-schooled in 1995 (up from 1,300 in 1990); in Saskatchewan, home schooling jumped from 730 in 1993 to 1,113 in 1996.[48]

Measuring System Performance

In addition to testing for the purposes of student evaluation, all but two jurisdictions have some form of provincial assessment program.[49] These system-wide assessments tend to focus on the basics — English or French as a first language and mathematics — although some provinces include science and social sciences. To obtain useful information for program development and improvement, provinces usually assess students at two or more levels, and subject areas on a rotating cycle.

The Atlantic provinces have joined forces under the Atlantic Provinces Education Foundation to analyze and report on student and system performance in Atlantic Canada. They have identified indicators in six areas: achievement, participation, cost of education, satisfaction, conditions of schooling, and lifelong learning.

In 1996, Ontario established the Education Quality and Accountability Office (EQAO), the only independent educational accountability agency in North America. Its job is to provide information about the quality of education and to identify and promote best practices. EQAO also undertakes provincial assessments of math, reading and writing in grades 3, 6 and 9.

---

[48] Council of Ministers of Education, Canada, *The Development of Education, op. cit.*, p. 33.

[49] Organisation for Economic Co-operation and Development, *Education at a Glance: OECD Indicators* (Paris: OECD, 1996), p. 262.

As a result of renewed interest in more systematic evaluation methods for Canada's school systems, the Council of Ministers of Education Canada launched its national School Achievement Indicators Program (SAIP) in 1993, to help provinces and territories assess student achievement and identify educational priorities in a national context.

In 1993, the first SAIP tests measured mathematical content and problem-solving in a random selection of 13- and 16-year olds across Canada. Reading and writing were assessed in 1994, followed by a science assessment in 1996 that measured two areas: knowledge of science concepts, and science inquiry and problem-solving.

Canadian students have participated in a number of international testing programs, including the international indicators project of the OECD, various studies of the International Assessment of Educational Progress (IAEP), and the International Association for the Evaluation of Educational Achievement (IEA).

In the Third International Mathematics and Science Study, which tested the achievement of grade 7 and 8 students in 50 countries under the auspices of the IEA, Canadian students placed above the international mean, at 59%. Students in British Columbia and Alberta stood out, at 63 and 61% respectively. Of the top ten countries with scores significantly higher than Canada's, four are Asian (Singapore, Japan, Korea, and Hong Kong), three are in Western Europe (Netherlands, Austria, and England), and three in Eastern or Central Europe (Czech Republic, Bulgaria and Slovenia).

Public Opinion

How Canadians feel about their school system depends on a number of factors: their age, their region or province, and whether or not they have children in school.

In a poll conducted by Environics in 1993, most Canadians gave their educational system a passing grade. Eight out of ten parents were satisfied with their own children's education, and almost as many were satisfied with current teaching methods. There was, however, a sense that the system is not as good as it once was. Although the poll revealed concerns about standards, seven out of ten respondents felt that society is more to blame for problems in education than teachers or school administrators, and that student success was determined more by home life than by school.

A 1994 Gallup poll was less positive. It found only 36% of Canadians satisfied with the education children are receiving, although satisfaction was higher among those with children under 18 in the home (41%). Satisfaction ranged from 24% in British Columbia to 43% in Atlantic Canada.

The Gallup poll also found more than 60% of Canadians in favour of more public spending on education. [50]

Teaching in Canada

The Workforce

More than a quarter of a million full-time teachers work in Canada's elementary and secondary schools. Between the mid 1980s and the early 1990s, the educator workforce increased by nearly 13%, while enrolment increased only 5%.[51] That growth rate began reversing itself in the mid 1990s, due to the combination of lower enrolments and political pressure for reduced public expenditures on education. By the middle of the decade, there was an overall surplus of teachers in Canada, although remote areas continue to have difficulty recruiting teachers.

Employment opportunities may open up over the next decade, as a large segment of the current teaching population reaches retirement age. More than 45% of teachers who were working in 1993 will be retired or near retirement by 2010.[52]

As recently as 1970, only 37% of Canadian elementary and secondary teachers held university degrees, and most of those were at the secondary level. Twenty years later, that proportion had risen to 80%.[53] Beginning in the 1970s, most provinces required a university degree as a prerequisite for teacher certification (with a few exceptions in non-academic subject areas). Thousands of teachers enrolled in full- or part-time university programs in the 1970s and 1980s to upgrade their qualifications, and the remaining non-degree teachers at the elementary level are approaching the end of their teaching careers.

---

[50] Council of Ministers of Education, Canada, *Enhancing the Role of Teachers in a Changing World* (Toronto: September 1996), pp. 21-22.

[51] Organisation for Economic Co-operation and Development, *Education at a Glance: OECD Indicators, op. cit.*, p. 262.

[52] Canadian Education Statistics Council, *Education Indicators in Canada, op. cit.*, p. 18.

[53] Canadian Education Statistics Council, *A Statistical Portrait, op. cit.*, p. 70.

Gender Issues in the Teaching Profession

Gender balance within the teaching profession has become an issue on two fronts: fair representation in administrative positions, and role-modelling as it relates to young people of both genders.

In 1982, women held 59.7% of all elementary and secondary teaching positions in Canada. A decade later, that had increased to 64.8%. In spite of their growing dominance in the workforce, women continue to be vastly under-represented at the administrative level — although they hold many positions of responsibility in supportive and consultative roles. In 1993, they still held only 30.5% of administrative positions (up from 17.7% a decade earlier), despite the fact that many provinces had established employment equity programs to address this imbalance.[54]

Gender imbalance is not only an issue of employment equity. Increasingly, it is being recognized as an educational issue in its own right. In addition to the imbalance in administrative positions, the conspicuous absence of women from science and technology fields at the secondary school level and the growing absence of men from elementary school classrooms leaves both male and female students without same-gender role models in significant areas of their school experience.

Teacher Education

Across Canada, almost 50 universities offer teacher certification programs, either as a one- or two-year post-degree bachelor of education program or as part of a four- or five-year university program (three years in Quebec). Professional training includes general and subject-related courses in teaching and learning, plus practical classroom experience. Those preparing to teach in the secondary system must have completed a specified number of university level courses in their subject area of specialization.

In most cases, departments and ministries of education review out-of-province credentials before issuing a teaching certificate. In British Columbia and Ontario this function has been taken over by Colleges of Teachers, self-regulating professional organizations.

Even though the demand for teachers has fallen, young people

---

[54] Council of Ministers of Education, Canada, *Enhancing the Role of Teachers, op. cit.*, p. 13.

continue to choose teaching as a career. Because of limited space in university programs, only a relatively small percentage of applicants are admitted to teacher education programs. Admission depends primarily on marks, although letters of reference, work experience and personal interviews are gaining importance in the screening process.[55]

Post-certification upgrading is not required by any province (although Nova Scotia has been considering a continual re-certification program), but many teachers achieve higher levels of certification by acquiring additional qualifications, usually through courses offered by departments of education, school boards and faculties of education. School boards sometimes subsidize additional training undertaken in the summer. In addition, local boards or schools may mandate in-service programs to meet particular provincial or local priorities, using the five to ten professional development days per year that each provincial department schedules. Teachers' federations, subject councils, and various educational institutions and organizations offer a variety of workshops, courses and conferences aimed at keeping teachers current with new developments in their fields.

Requirements for administrative positions vary. Some boards require principals to hold a master's degree in educational administration or curriculum. Ontario requires both vice-principals and principals to obtain a principal's certificate.

Working Conditions

Teacher salaries depend on a combination of education and years of experience. Teachers are placed in a category based on educational level. Pay increases are usually automatic for the first seven to 14 years of employment, at which point teachers reach the maximum salary level for their category. From that point, increases are limited to those achieved in the collective bargaining process.

Salary scales show considerable variability from province to province. The frequent and substantial salary increases which characterized the 1970s and 1980s have fallen victim to fiscal restraint. In the mid-90s, starting salaries for teachers with minimum degree standing ranged from approximately $25,000 to $35,000, and maximum salaries from $35,000 to $56,000. For teachers with at least five years of post-

---

[55] Council of Ministers of Education, Canada, *The Development of Education, op. cit.*, p. 50.

secondary education, minimums ranged from approximately $28,000 to $38,000, and maximums from $41,000 to $65,000. In both Yukon and the Northwest Territories, salaries were substantially higher.[56]

Teacher workload is often measured by pupil:teacher ratio (PTR). This is a crude measure, because it includes all educators in the system as well as classroom teachers, but it is a commonly used indicator of workload and class size trends. Since 1982, the national pupil:educator ratio, in elementary and secondary schools, has decreased from 18.4 to less than 16.[57] Like salary levels, PTRs (which are really a measure of educator numbers) stabilized during the period of retrenchment in the 1990s.

The average workload of full-time teachers has been increasing from 39.4 hours per week in 1982 to 40.9 hours per week ten years later. This increase is not spread evenly across the country; over the 10-year period, teachers in Alberta and Quebec increased their hours on the job by 3 and 2.2 hours, respectively.[58]

Teachers are represented by unions, or federations, in all provinces. In some cases, a single union represents all teachers; in others, elementary and secondary teachers are represented by separate unions; in still others, separate and public school teachers are organized separately; and in Ontario, men and women in English language public schools at the elementary level had separate unions until membership by gender was challenged in the courts. These two federations are now in the process of amalgamating. Ontario also has a French language teachers' association at the elementary level.

---

[56] Council of Ministers of Education, Canada, *Enhancing the Role of Teachers, op. cit.*, p. 15.

[57] Council of Ministers of Education, Canada, *The Development of Education, op. cit.*, p. 49.

[58] *Ibid.*, p. 47.

Chapter 2

POST-SECONDARY EDUCATION IN CANADA

Higher Education: Investing in the Future

> *Our economy has developed to the point at which post-secondary education and training have become the keys to survival in the job market, surely a sign of a knowledge based economy.*[1]

CANADIANS can choose from a wide range of post-secondary institutions and programs, available in 88 universities and more than 200 community colleges. More than 1.4 million post-secondary students enrol in college and university programs every year, placing Canada second only to the United States in its higher education participation rate.[2] Post-secondary education includes academic programs above the high school level, technical education, and applied arts and sciences. Trade and vocational training programs are also available to students of post-secondary age, but they are not, strictly speaking, post-secondary programs since they do not usually require secondary school completion.

Post-secondary education has become an important component

---

[1] Association of Community Colleges in Canada (ACCC), "Post-Secondary Education in the Knowledge Economy: Submission to the Senate Sub-committee on Post-secondary Education," January 1997 (www.accc.ca., accessed 3/18/97).

[2] Human Resources Development Canada (HRDC), *Federal and Provincial Support to Post-Secondary Education in Canada: A Report to Parliament 1995-96* (Ottawa: Supply and Services Canada, 1997), p. 27.

of the nation's economic policy. As the 21st century approaches, most Canadians agree with these words from the federal government's 1991 discussion paper, *Learning Well...Living Well:* "If we wish to maintain our prosperity, we must build on our past performance in education and invest as effectively as possible in the development of our people. A highly qualified work force is essential to ensure that all Canadians have better employment opportunities, more employment security and higher wages."[3]

Post-secondary Education in Canada: A Short History

Until the end of World War II, post-secondary education in Canada was synonymous with university education. Université Laval, founded in 1663 as the Séminaire de Québec, is among the oldest universities in North America. The University of New Brusnwick, Canada's oldest English language institution, opened in 1785. By the time of Confederation, Canada boasted 17 colleges — all of them small, denominational, elitist institutions which focused on the liberal arts.

In the early 20th century, the four western provinces — following the lead of the United States — established publicly funded, provincially chartered universities with more liberal admission policies. But east of Manitoba, universities continued to be "selective and conservative, reflecting their church-related origins."[4] Provincial governments operated a few vocational and agricultural institutions.

The federal government began committing resources to post-secondary studies during and immediately after World War I, when it first established the National Research Council as a war-time research base, and then introduced and educational assistance plan for returning veterans. But at that time, neither the public nor the government saw university education as an appropriate area for significant public investment. It was not until after World War II that Ottawa began making a "sustained and concerted effort" to support higher education and research. The Veterans' Rehabilitation Act of 1945 was accompanied by a gradually increasing commitment of federal funds, first through direct grants and later through transfers to the provinces

---

[3] *Learning Well...Living Well* (Ottawa: Prosperity Secretariat, Supply and Services, Canada, 1991), p. xi.

[4] John Dennison and Paul Gallagher, *Canada's Community Colleges: A Critical Analysis* (Vancouver: University of British Columbia Press, 1986), p. 1.

to help defray university operating costs. During the immediate post-war years, the federal government also became a primary sponsor of university-based research.[5]

In the 1960s, several factors combined to create an explosion in post-secondary education. The post-war baby boom, which had already made its mark on elementary and secondary schools, was rapidly approaching university age. In 1960, university and college enrolments totalled 120,000, with projected enrolments of 250,000 for 1967, and more than 350,000 for 1970. At the same time, social factors were creating a new sense of entitlement to post-secondary education. Canada's closer alliance with the United States was nudging it away from the British, hierarchical education system towards a more egalitarian approach with an emphasis on equal access. The western provinces, with their affinity to the United States, had already led the way in that transition. Scientific and technical changes following the war were also feeding the explosion by creating a new demand for higher education. And finally, but perhaps most importantly, the nation's post-war economic engine depended on an increasingly educated workforce. "In fact, the prospect of further economic development for Canada drove educational expansion. A belief in the return on investment in post-secondary education, for both individual Canadians and for Canadian society as a whole, really motivated government action in education with full concurrence of the electorate."[6]

Following the recommendations of the Royal Commission on National Development in the Arts, Letters, and Sciences (the Massey Commission), the federal government began granting funds directly to universities in 1951. In 1967, with the passage of the *Federal-Provincial Fiscal Arrangements Act*, the federal government began reimbursing the provinces for 50% of their higher education operating costs, and extended its support to include academic and technical programs in both the university and non-university sectors. This extension of federal involvement allowed provinces to embark on an unprecedented period of expansion.

As enrolment more than doubled between 1955 and 1962, and then doubled again by 1969, new post-secondary institutions sprang up from coast to coast. Nineteen new universities were granted provincial charters, and a network of new institutions, commonly

---

[5] Association of Universities and Colleges in Canada (AUCC), "Canadian Higher Education: An Overview" in *The Directory of Canadian Universities, 1996-1997/ Le Répertoire des universités canadiennes*, 31st ed. (Ottawa: AUCC, 1996), p. vi.

[6] John Dennison and Paul Gallagher, *op. cit.*, pp. 12-14, 82.

Post-secondary Education in Canada

called community colleges, was established to satisfy the growing need for skilled technical workers. The mandate of these colleges was to meet both the educational needs of vocationally oriented secondary school graduates and the labour needs of those who would employ them — industry, business, health and public service sectors. Community colleges offered a range of advanced programs as an alternative to traditional university degree programs.

By the 1980s, the hey-day of post-secondary expansion had passed. Canadians were facing a prolonged period of fiscal restraint at all levels. Although student enrolments remained high, public support for the system was waning in the face of a poor economy, high unemployment rates, and a pervasive skepticism about all government expenditures. Retrenchment became the order of the day. Although support at both levels of government has remained substantial, both colleges and universities have experienced major funding cuts from both levels of government, especially in the 1990s.

Still, if numbers tell the tale, individual Canadians continue to believe in higher education as a worthwhile investment. The following statistics show that post-secondary participation rates have stayed high despite economic uncertainty. However, behind the statistics lies a growing concern about the ability of institutions (particularly universities) to adapt to reduced public support and the changing employment market, and the ability of students to pay ever-increasing fees.

Enrolment Patterns and Program Choices

The OECD ranks Canada highest among member nations for the percentage of its population which has completed a post-secondary program. Some 13% of Canadians hold a university degree, and another 25% have at least one post-secondary certificate or diploma.[7] In the 25-34 age group, 51% of Canadians hold a degree or diploma, compared to 32% of Americans. In the 45 - 54 age group, 45% of Canadians, compared to 33% of Americans, have completed a post-secondary program.[8]

Even after the population bulge of the 1960s and 1970s passed

---

[7] Statistics Canada, *Canada at a Glance 1996), op. cit.*, p. 5.
[8] Organisation for Economic Co-operation and Development (OECD), *Education at a Glance: Analysis* (Paris: OECD, 1996), p. 68.

through the system, university enrolments continued to climb, dropping off marginally for the first time in 1995. Since the 1970s, the number of university graduates has increased steadily until, by the mid-1990s, more than 100,000 degrees were being granted every year. The great majority of these are bachelor's degrees or first professional degrees; the proportion of graduate degrees has been stable at 12-13% for master's degrees and 2% for doctorates. In 1995, 577,800 students were enrolled full-time in university degree programs.[9]

Much of the growth in university enrolment figures can be explained by the increased participation rate of women, which has nearly doubled since 1980. More than half of all post-secondary students are now women. A study of student choices between 1983 and 1993 found that the proportion of women increased in every university program and at every level, except in education (where they already dominated), including the traditionally male-dominated science programs. The gender gap is narrowing, but it has not closed. Men continue to outnumber women in engineering, forestry, computer science, meteorology, and the physical sciences.[10]

In the college system, the number of graduates has gradually increased from approximately 60,000 per year in the mid-1970s to approximately 80,000 per year in the mid-1980s. It has remained relatively stable since that time.[11] In 1995, 388,600 students were enrolled full-time in diploma or certificate programs in over 200 community colleges.[12]

The proportion of men and women in college programs remained unchanged over the decade between 1983 and 1993, but their program choices shifted. Women's enrolment increased in arts and natural sciences and decreased in health, engineering, business and commerce.[13] Men continued to outnumber women in electronics, transportational technologies, general and mechanical engineering, environment and conservation.

Overall, students choosing social sciences over engineering and applied science increased at both the college and university levels. In 1996, the Conference Board of Canada expressed concern that "Canada, like Australia and the United States, has a much larger share of graduates in the humanities than Sweden, Germany, Norway or

---

[9] Statistics Canada, *Canada at a Glance 1996, op. cit.*
[10] Canadian Education Statistics Council (CESC), *Education Indicators in Canada* (Toronto: CESC, 1996), p. 86.
[11] *Ibid.*, p. 114.
[12] Statistics Canada, *Canada at a Glance 1996, op. cit.*, p. 5.
[13] CESC, *Education Indicators in Canada, op. cit.*, p. 86.

Post-secondary Education in Canada

Japan. In 1992, 52% of Canada's degrees were in the humanities, compared with only 7% in engineering; Japan in contrast, granted 22% of its degrees in engineering. Science degrees are also under-represented in Canada."[14]

However, the sixth annual issue of *Maclean's* on Canadian universities (1996) speaks of a "slow but unmistakable shift toward more practical programs," and reports that nationwide university enrolments in political science, English and history dropped between 1991 and 1994, after a decade of growth, while enrolments in nursing, computer science and environmental studies grew.[15]

The graphs on page 53 show the range of programs available in universities and colleges as well as changes in enrolment levels and gender distribution between 1984 and 1995.

Most Canadians continue to see post-secondary education as a full-time occupation for 18 - 22 year olds, but in fact that pattern is changing. More older students are joining the ranks at both colleges and universities, and part-time study is the preferred option of many, especially at the college level. Approximately 25% of all post-secondary students, and more than 50% of part-time students, are now over 24 years of age.[16] More students are delaying their entry into post-secondary programs, remaining in school longer, and alternating post-secondary education with work and family responsibilities.

The move to part-time study has affected colleges more than universities. In 1992-93, 27% of college students combined part-time study with other activities, 6% more than a decade earlier. According to the Association of Community Colleges of Canada, almost 1.5 million Canadians are engaged in part-time studies at a local community colleges or technical institutes. In contrast, universities reported a significant reduction in part-time enrolments between 1994 and 1995.[17] Some speculate that rising fees, along with other financial reasons and changes in the labour market, are discouraging students from part-time university study, but it is too early to identify a clear trend.

Many students at both college and university combine work and study. Forty per cent of full-time students work part-time; more than three-quarters of part-time students hold jobs. Most spend between 10

---

[14] Conference Board of Canada, as quoted in "Post-secondary Education," ACCC, *op. cit.*, p. 7.

[15] "A Crash Course in Reality 101," *Maclean's*, 25 November 1996, p. 52.

[16] CMEC, *The Development of Education: Report of Canada* (Toronto: CMEC, 1996), p. 36.

[17] ACCC, "Post-secondary Education,"*op. cit.*; and CESC, *Education Indicators, op. cit.*, p. 84.

Post-secondary Education in Canada

Full-time Enrolment in University Undergraduate Programs, by Field of Study and Gender, Canada, 1983-84 and 1994-95

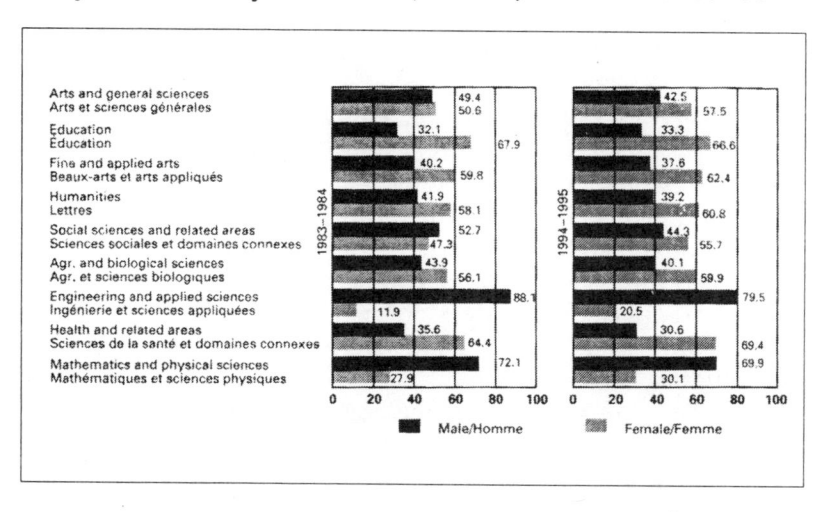

Field of Study	1983-1984 Male	1983-1984 Female	1994-1995 Male	1994-1995 Female
Arts and general sciences / Arts et sciences générales	49.4	50.6	42.5	57.5
Education / Éducation	32.1	67.9	33.3	66.6
Fine and applied arts / Beaux-arts et arts appliqués	40.2	59.8	37.6	62.4
Humanities / Lettres	41.9	58.1	39.2	60.8
Social sciences and related areas / Sciences sociales et domaines connexes	52.7	47.3	44.3	55.7
Agr. and biological sciences / Agr. et sciences biologiques	43.9	56.1	40.1	59.9
Engineering and applied sciences / Ingénierie et sciences appliquées	88.1	11.9	79.5	20.5
Health and related areas / Sciences de la santé et domaines connexes	35.6	64.4	30.6	69.4
Mathematics and physical sciences / Mathématiques et sciences physiques	72.1	27.9	69.9	30.1

Full-time Enrolment in Community College Career Programs, by Field of Study and Gender, Canada, 1983-84 and 1992-93

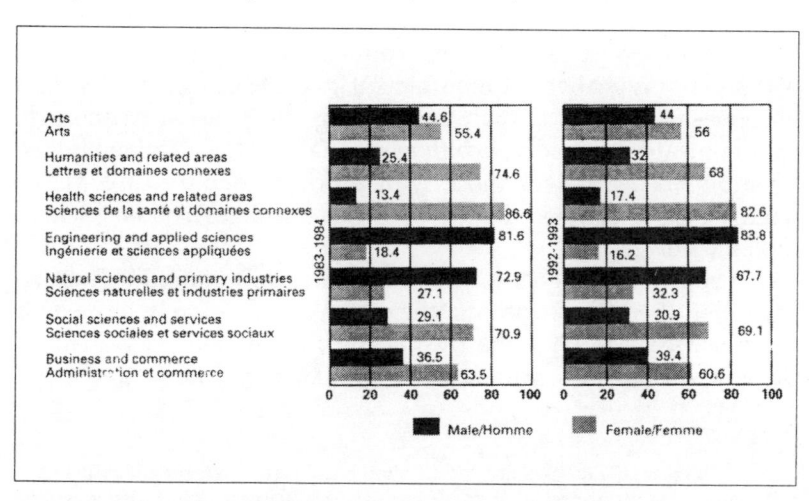

Field of Study	1983-1984 Male	1983-1984 Female	1992-1993 Male	1992-1993 Female
Arts / Arts	44.6	55.4	44	56
Humanities and related areas / Lettres et domaines connexes	25.4	74.6	32	68
Health sciences and related areas / Sciences de la santé et domaines connexes	13.4	86.6	17.4	82.6
Engineering and applied sciences / Ingénierie et sciences appliquées	81.6	18.4	83.8	16.2
Natural sciences and primary industries / Sciences naturelles et industries primaires	72.9	27.1	67.7	32.3
Social sciences and services / Sciences sociales et services sociaux	29.1	70.9	30.9	69.1
Business and commerce / Administration et commerce	36.5	63.5	39.4	60.6

Source: Canadian Education Statistics Council, *Indicators* (Ottawa and Toronto: CESC, 1996), p. 87, graphs 5.3a and 5.3b.

and 14 hours per week at work, but one in five works 20 hours a week or more.[18]

Native Student Participation

The federal Department of Indian Affairs and Northern Development encourages Native participation in full-time and part-time post-secondary study by providing financial assistance to eligible Indian and Inuit students directly through the federal government's Post-secondary Student Support Program. In 1994-95, nearly 27,000 Indian and Inuit students were enrolled in post-secondary institutions, up from 8,000 in 1983-84. More than half were in undergraduate university programs; the remainder were working toward diplomas or certificates.

Study areas which attract the highest concentration of Native students are general arts and sciences, social sciences, business and commerce, and education. Participation rates are lowest in agriculture and biological sciences, mathematics, and physical sciences.[19]

Personal Benefits of Post-Secondary Education

Despite labour market uncertainty and rising fees, the motivation to pursue post-secondary education remains high. As the needs of the economy change, the requirement for post-secondary education is increasing — especially in the growing industries of technology, communications, finance, health and social services. Nationally, the unemployment rate for those with a post-secondary diploma or degree is 6.5%, compared to 8.5% for those with a secondary school diploma only.[20]

People with higher education are not only more likely to be employed than those without, they are also more likely to be high wage earners. In 1993, the median income for all individuals in Canada was $20,666, compared to $24,002 for those with a post-

---

[18] *Ibid.*, p. 62.

[19] "Increase in Post-Secondary Education Enrolment," *Facts from Stats: Information Quality and Research Directorate Information Management Branch.* Issue No. 9, December-January 1996. (http://www.inac.gc.ca/stats/facts/possec.html)

[20] "Education at a Glance," *Education Quarterly Review 1996*, vol. 3, no. 4 (1996), p. 54.

secondary certificate or diploma, and $34,815 for university graduates. The only exception to the positive correlation between level of education and level of income appears to be those who begin post-secondary education but do not complete their programs. Their incomes fall substantially below the median, probably because they are disproportionately employed part-time or part-year. (Median income increases with age for all groups, so youth incomes are always lowest.)[21]

Post-secondary education also increases the probability that employment will relate to the student's field of study. The "education/job match" is greatest with the most highly educated; 75% of Ph.D.s report that they are working in their field (primarily as professors). Specialized career/technology training (community college level) ranks second, at 67%. Approximately 58% of university graduates report a direct relationship between their education and their jobs. Like incomes, education/job match increases over time, so that even when young workers begin in jobs unrelated to their education, they are not likely to become trapped there.[22] According to two studies tracking university graduates in Alberta and British Columbia, arts majors are least likely to find a job that matches their academic studies. When compared with other graduates, they also have among the lowest median incomes.[23]

Responding to Change

Post-secondary education is under the microscope in Canada. A changing job market, stubbornly high rates of unemployment, and a fiscal environment characterized by government cuts to all services are leading many provinces and the federal government to look for ways to make college and university education more relevant, accessible, and affordable. As a result, reviews and reforms are under way in a number of jurisdictions.

The Senate of Canada Committee on Social Affairs, Science and Technology began a review of post-secondary education in June 1996. It is focusing on education quality, student accessibility to institutions outside their own region, student aid, research funding, and international opportunities for Canadian universities and colleges.

---

[21] CESC, *Education Indicators, op. cit.,* p. 128.
[22] *Ibid.,* p. 126.
[23] "A Crash Course in Reality 101," *op. cit.,* pp. 51-52.

The governments of Manitoba, Ontario, Alberta, Newfoundland, and British Columbia have all put post-secondary education on their agenda for change.

Manitoba has introduced a formal, co-ordinated system of planning and budgeting through a Council on Post-secondary Education. The council will bring universities and colleges together under a single body, which will examine joint programs and look for ways to improve access, portability and accountability.

The Ontario government established a panel to examine costs, efficiency and accessibility issues, and to explore the possibility of allowing private universities and colleges to compete with existing institutions. Its report, which was published in December 1996, recommended a less regulated environment for Ontario universities and colleges, including the freedom of individual institutions to set their own fees. It also recommended that the province increase its financial commitment to post-secondary education.

Alberta has developed a funding mechanism for post-secondary institutions which is based on performance. The province will evaluate colleges and universities according to a set of indicators — including student satisfaction, employment rate of graduates, cost factors, and research — and will add funds to operating grants according to outcomes.

As a cost-saving measure, Newfoundland has merged its five regional colleges into a single provincial college. Certain of the existing campuses will take on a provincial co-ordinating role for specialized areas of programming.

British Columbia has adopted a strategic plan to improve post-secondary relevance and accessibility. The government has addressed the issue of accessibility by promising to increase student spaces and freeze student fees. Program initiatives include a provincial electronic learning network, more flexible scheduling, reducing barriers to non-traditional students, and encouraging partnerships with business and industry for retraining and upgrading workers.

Portability of Courses and Credits

Students enrolling in Canadian colleges and universities may have have difficulty receiving full recognition for courses taken at institution. Several provinces have developed credit-transfer agreements between community colleges and universities which allow students to apply credits gained at one institution toward a degree or diploma from another. The Council of Ministers has spearheaded the Pan-Canadian Protocol on the Transferability of University Credits to encourage universities to recognize first- and second-year courses granted by other institutions (including the university transfer courses in community colleges). Most have agreed to the protocol, and the CMEC is working with the provinces to extend it to the final two years of undergraduate study. Nova Scotia has already implemented a policy of full transferability for first- and second-year courses within the Nova Scotia university system, and the University of Prince Edward Island now recognizes credits from any university in Canada.[24]

The issue of portability reaches beyond the ability of individual students to transfer credits and change institutions to the structure of post-secondary programs themselves. The Maritime Provinces Higher Education Commission, for example, has issued guidelines to assist universities and community colleges to develop joint, or "articulated" programs, which blend academic study with technical, applied study, and grant joint diplomas or degrees.

Canadian Universities

Canada's universities range from the very large, with a full selection of undergraduate and graduate degree programs, to small liberal arts colleges, affiliated denominational colleges, and specialized professional institutes. With few exceptions, they are publicly funded. Students can choose to study in cities, small towns, or on the electronic highway. The term university is usually used to indicate degree-granting authority, but some smaller degree-granting institutions call themselves colleges or institutes. This creates occasional confusion, since community colleges in Canada do not grant degrees.

Admission Requirements and Programs of Study

Although every university sets its own admission standards, institutions in the same province usually have the same requirements,

---

[24] CMEC, *The Development of Education, op. cit.*, p. 41.

particularly for undergraduate arts and sciences programs. Although the majority of students choose to attend university within their own province, nothing prevents them from attending anywhere within Canada.

Most students enter university directly from secondary school, except in Quebec, where they first complete two years at a *collège d'enseignement général et professionnel (cégep)*. Ontario students must complete six Ontario Academic Credits (OACs) to be admitted to university. In all other provinces and territories, students enter university after completion of grade 12. When the number of applicants exceeds the spaces available in a particular program, universities select those students with the highest academic performance in secondary school. Average high-school marks of incoming first-year university students vary from one university to another, and from program to program within universities. In 1995, they ranged from 73% to 87%.[25]

Special admission procedures are usually available for mature students who do not meet the normal entrance requirements.

Universities offer a broad range of programs in the arts, sciences, social sciences, engineering and applied sciences, leading to degrees at the bachelor's, master's, and doctorate (Ph.D.) levels. A few specialize in programs like fine arts, agriculture, education or theology. Some smaller universities (sometimes called colleges) offer only undergraduate programs. First-year students usually select a program area at the time of application, but may wait until they have begun their program to choose a subject major. The flexibility that individual students have to choose courses and to change areas of study varies from university to university, and within program areas and majors.

Each university sets its own degree requirements. Some grant a bachelor's degree at the pass (general) level after three years (or equivalent), and require a fourth year for an honours degree. Others require four years for both degrees, with more advanced courses or a higher achievement level for the honours degree. First professional degrees (e.g., engineering, business administration, education, journalism) are also awarded at the bachelor's level, and require either four years after secondary school, or an additional one or two years after an undergraduate degree. Students wishing to pursue graduate studies must complete undergraduate work at the honours level.

A master's degree requires at least one full year of study, and is usually required before Ph.D. study begins. A Ph.D. can sometimes be

---

[25] "Reading the Rankings, "*Maclean's*, 25 November 1996, p. 36.

completed with an additional two years of full-time study, but frequently requires longer. Ph.D. candidates must spend one full year on campus, and must usually research, write, and defend a thesis (a major paper based on original research). Most professional programs, such as law, medicine, or veterinary schools, require students to complete prerequisite university courses and write specialized entrance tests.

Many universities also offer a range of certificate and diploma courses in professional fields like health science, agriculture, and business at both the undergraduate and graduate level.

Language of Instruction

The language of instruction in most Canadian universities outside Quebec is English, although many offer some courses in French, and at some French-speaking students can write papers and exams in French. Sixteen French-language and three English-language universities operate in Quebec, where 85% of the population is French-speaking. The Université de Moncton (New Brunswick), with three campuses, is the largest French-language university in North America outside Quebec. In Nova Scotia, the Université Sainte-Anne, in Manitoba, the Collège universitaire de Saint-Boniface and in Alberta, the Faculté Saint-Jean at the University of Alberta, serve francophone students as well.[26] The University of Ottawa, Laurentian University and its affiliate, Collège de Hearst, and the Glendon campus of York University are bilingual institutions in Ontario.

School Year

Most Canadian universities operate on a two-semester year, from September to May. Some are on a trimester system, with most courses available throughout the year.

Tuition Fees

University costs are a major issue for Canadians, who have come to expect university education to be accessible to all who qualify. Provincial governments set fee structures, which vary from one province to another. Even within provinces, fees may vary somewhat from one university to another, and from one faculty to another — but

---

[26] CMEC, *The Development of Education, op. cit.*, p. 35.

they have been rising everywhere as government contributions have been falling. Fees have climbed in the past ten years, and now average approximately $3000 per year.[27] Tuition fees represent only 25-35% of the total cost to students when books, living expenses, travel and incidentals are included.

On average, student fees now account for about one-quarter of university operating revenues (compared to 13% in 1980).[28] In Ontario, they now account for about 35%.

Canadian students are eligible for financial assistance, based on need, from the Canada, Quebec, and the Northwest Territories Student Loan Plans and from provincial student assistance programs. However, recent shifts away from outright grants to student loans, combined with higher tuition fees, leave a good percentage of Canadian students forced to take loans.

Most universities also provide scholarships to students based on academic performance or need. At the graduate (master's and doctorate) levels, a variety of fellowships, assistantships and grants help to defray student costs.

All provinces, except Newfoundland, Saskatchewan and Manitoba, set higher fees for foreign students. In 1996-97, Ontario deregulated tuition fees for foreign students. Ontario colleges and universities now set the fees for these students. A number of universities offer free tuition to senior citizens.

Tuition Fees 1996-1997*

	Canadian Students		Foreign Students	
	Undergraduate	Graduate	Undergraduate	Graduate
British Columbia	$2,258-$7,860	$2,100-$2,898	$3,475-$7,860	$2,100-$2,898
Alberta	$2,789-$4,834	$2,352-$6,507	$4,590-$6,446	$4,365-$13,000
Saskatchewan	$2,640-$2,670	$2,640-3,338	$5,280-$5,738	$3,338-$5,280
Manitoba	$2,296-$3,033	$3,131-$3,388	$3,575-$4,590	$3,131-$5,929
Ontario	$2,816-$2,986	$1,286-$4,422	$6,100-$11,096	$2,211-$15,312
Quebec	$1,665-$1,840	$1,482-$1,925	$7,453-7,630	$7,453-$10,605
New Brunswick	$2,420-$3,665	$500-$2,880	$4,120-$7,198	$2,450-$4,880
Nova Scotia	$3,210-$4,026	$2,825-$5,950	$5,100-$7,205	$5,100-$8,650
Prince Edward Is.	$2,920	$1,920	$4,620-$6,320	$3,620-$5,320
Newfoundland	$2,670	$1,641-$3,072	$5,340	$1,641-$3,072

* Fees in Canadian dollars for general arts or science.

Source: AUCC/Statistics Canada, 1997.

---

[27] AUCC, "Canadian Higher Education," *op. cit.*, p. ix.
[28] *Ibid.*, p. viii.

Accommodation

On-campus residences and meal plans are usually available at reasonable cost. However, few universities have enough on-campus housing to guarantee space after the first year, and many students move off-campus into apartments or other shared accommodation.

University Governance

The provincial charters which establish universities allow them to grant degrees and function as relatively autonomous institutions. Provincial governments usually restrict their involvement to finances, fee structures, and expansion into major new program areas. Most universities govern themselves under a bicameral system, in which a board of governors takes ultimate responsibility for finance and policy decisions, and a faculty senate makes academic decisions about program, admission requirements, degree requirements and academic planning. Senate recommendations are subject to final approval by the board, which usually defers to the senate's wishes.

In most cases, both the province and the university appoint members to the board. The province ensures that the institution's various constituencies are represented, while the university itself is represented by elected faculty and students, with administrators sitting as ex-officio members. The senate consists primarily of elected faculty members with, increasingly, representation from students.

Only federated colleges or universities are fully empowered to administer themselves and grant their own degrees. Affiliated colleges or universities are self-administrating institutions without degree-granting authority; they grant the degrees of their parent institutions. Constituent institutions grant degrees of a parent college or university, and are subject to its administrative control as well.

Universities are usually organized into several faculties, or broad program areas, presided over by deans — for example, a faculty of the arts, including humanities and social sciences, and a faculty of science, including pure physical and biological sciences. Faculties themselves are further subdivided into academic departments, headed by a member of the teaching staff. University instructors and professors are expected to spend a portion of their time in governance-related activities at the department or faculty level.

Faculty associations have become unionized in most universities, and negotiate collective agreements with their individual institutions.

In some provinces, organizations or associations of universities act as advisory intermediary bodies between the institutions and the provincial government. The Newfoundland and Labrador Council on Higher Education, the Saskatchewan Post-secondary Advisory Council, the Maritime Provinces Higher Education Commission, and Quebec's Conseil supérieur de l'éducation are examples of such bodies. They provide advice to government on financial and broad program issues. Some, like Manitoba's Post-secondary Education Council and the Nova Scotia Council on Higher Education, have the power to make decisions themselves.[29]

New Calls for Accountability

There are no national standards or accreditation procedures for Canadian universities. Membership in the Association of Universities and Colleges of Canada (AUCC) is deemed to indicate that institutions are meeting acceptable standards, but in fact universities in Canada, as elsewhere in the world, rest on the strength of their academic credentials and reputation. University and professional associations occasionally act as overseers of quality.

But universities have not escaped the growing public pressure for accountability. The *Maclean's* annual ranking of Canadian universities is one highly visible response to that pressure. It divides universities into three categories: medical/doctoral, with a broad range of Ph.D. programs and research, including medical schools; comprehensive, with significant research activity and a broad range of programs, including professional degrees, at the graduate and undergraduate levels; and primarily undergraduate, focusing on undergraduate education with relatively few graduate programs. Universities within these three categories are ranked according to criteria like average grades of incoming students, class sizes, faculty degrees and awards, allocation of available funds, size of library, and reputation among graduates and within the community. The results are frequently controversial, and some universities debate the choice and weighting of criteria, but the annual publication has raised the public profile of Canada's university system.

Ultimately, universities are accountable to those who pay for them and use them. The concept of market-driven higher education is relatively new in Canada, and highly controversial; but in the current climate of government cutbacks and high unemployment, it is taking

---

[29] CMEC, *The Development of Education, op. cit.*, p. 37.

root rapidly. In some instances, universities are allowing traditional programs to lapse if they are not cost-effective; they are allowing academic program funding to fluctuate according to enrolment or specific economic demand; and they are setting full cost-recovery fees for specialized programs. Ontario is considering allowing private universities to compete with public institutions; Alberta is using "key performance indicators" to determine future funding levels. To some, these moves are an overdue attempt to match higher education with the demands of a changing economy. To others, they are a red flag, warning that universities risk sacrificing their freedom and academic excellence for short-term economic objectives.[30] Whether they are perceived as a force for good or ill, market forces are unquestionably altering Canada's university system as it approaches the 21st century.

Teaching in Canadian Universities

The *Maclean's* ranking of universities measures the university teaching environment by two standards: the number of tenured and tenure-stream faculty teaching first-year classes (as opposed to graduate students and short-term or part-time instructors), and the size of classes. In 1996, it found the percentage of first-year classes taught by tenured faculty at each university ranged widely, from 35 at one extreme to 85 at the other. There was little difference among the three categories of universities (medical/doctoral, comprehensive and primarily undergraduate).

Virtually no Canadian universities reported class sizes of over 500, and very few over 250. Most have some classes exceeding 100, mainly in first- and second-year courses, but the majority of classes in all institutions have 50 or fewer students.[31]

A Tradition of Research

Scholarly research and teaching are seen as complementary activities in most Canadian universities — in arts and humanities, as well as in pure, applied and social sciences.

"Canadian university researchers have a long record of success: from the discovery of insulin and the development of pablum in the 1920s to the more recent development of plastics that biodegrade in the sun. University researchers have developed canola into Canada's

---
[30] "A Crash Course in Reality 101,"*op. cit.*, p. 54.
[31] "Reading the Rankings, "*op. cit.*, pp. 40-41.

third largest crop, invented the world's first artificial pancreas, identified the gene that causes cystic fibrosis, developed the electronic pacemaker and ultra-precise satellite navigation and surveying systems. They've been the first to synthesize RNA, built the first commercial electron microscope and found new ways to help people cope with pain and stress."[32]

Governments — federal and provincial — fund the majority of university-based research. Federal government support for basic and applied research is funnelled through three research granting councils: Medical Research Council, Natural Sciences and Engineering Research Council, and Social Sciences and Humanities Research Council. These councils operate at arm's length from government, with a mandate to foster a strong research base, link university research activities to Canada's economic and social priorities, and develop highly qualified research personnel. Eight provinces have established similar agencies to support provincially-funded research programs.

Although most university-based research is basic research, cooperative efforts between universities and industry are on the rise. Research is becoming more focused on the "strategic areas required for Canada's social and economic health," and more universities are establishing separate research facilities to foster partnerships and to move the results of their research findings into the private sector. This joint activity has a significant spin-off for the Canadian economy. The National Sciences and Engineering Research Council and the National Research Council recently studied the economic impact of companies established by universities or university researchers to commercialize inventions resulting directly from research funded by these councils. They found 8,000 - 10,000 people employed directly and estimated a combined spin-off of more than $1 billion annually.

In 1993, business investment in university research stood at $270 million, three times the 1988 level. Although this is an encouraging trend, Canada's national research and development performance is still lower than most OECD countries, and its industrial investment in research is only half the OECD average.[33]

---

[32] AUCC, "Canadian Higher Education,"*op. cit.*, p. vii.
[33] *Ibid.*

Canada's Community College System

Canada's network of community colleges includes 200 institutions with numerous campuses in every province and territory. Community colleges vary in size, but the average college has approximately 5,000 full-time and 15,000 part-time students.[34]

Although many were established in the 1960s, some community colleges have roots which reach back much farther as technical and vocational training institutions. Their primary mandate is to offer semi-professional career and technical education or vocational programs leading to employment. Their character and designation vary somewhat from province to province: colleges of applied arts and technology in Ontario; colleges of general and vocational education in Quebec; technical/vocational and university-oriented colleges in British Columbia, Alberta and Yukon; and colleges providing specialized training in areas like agriculture, the arts, marine technology, and paramedical technology.

The distinction between universities and community colleges has blurred somewhat in recent years. Community colleges award diplomas and certificates rather than degrees, but many also offer courses for transfer to the university system. Some universities and community colleges are entering into joint program arrangements, combining academic and applied studies under a single program. And in recent years, a growing number of university graduates have been attending community college after completing their university studies, in order to acquire a vocational skill for employment.

While universities debate their appropriate relationship to employment opportunities and the private sector, colleges are clear: their primary function is to prepare students to take advantage of current employment trends in their province or region. In fact, one distinguishing characteristic of community colleges is their linkage with business and industry, and their integrated role in regional economic development.

---

[34] ACCC, *Getting to Know Us*. (Broadsheet.)

Admission Requirements and Programs of Study

Open access is a hallmark of Canada's community colleges. They operate on the philosophy that educational opportunities should be available to a broad segment of society. As a result, their admission criteria are flexible. Secondary school graduation is usually required, but the requirement may be waived in the case of mature applicants or in special circumstances; unlike universities, colleges do not evaluate potential applicants on the basis of previous academic performance. When the number of applicants exceeds available spaces, students are admitted by lottery or on a first-come, first-serve basis. Although entry requirements are often flexible, students are expected to meet institutional standards in order to receive a diploma.

Quebec's General and Vocational Colleges (called "cégeps" after their French title, *collèges d'enseignement général et professionnel*) have a unique dual mandate. They offer two distinct programs: a two-year general education program leading to university, and a three-year technical or career program leading to employment.

With the exception of university-bound students in Quebec, most students who attend community college enrol in a career or technical program. In *Canada's Community Colleges,* Dennison and Gallagher describe these programs like this: "career, technical, and para-professional programmes of bewildering variety, of two or three years duration, intended to prepare graduates for employment at technical, mid-managerial, or professional assistant levels." The programs usually place special emphasis on new areas of employment in fields as diverse as business, health sciences, social service, cultural arts, public safety and criminology, medical technologies and recreation.[35]

Community colleges work closely with local employers and government agencies to project manpower requirements and design programs to meet projected employment needs in the region. As a result of this regional focus, specific programs vary considerably from one college to another.

All community colleges offer a variety of job-training and general interest courses which are not considered post-secondary. They are discussed in Chapter Three.

---

[35] John Dennison and Paul Gallagher, *op. cit.*, p. 71.

School Year

The school year in community colleges takes several forms. Most follow a semester system similar to the universities', from September through May. Some use a trimester system, with three equal terms. A few operate on a September to June calendar, similar to elementary and secondary schools.

Language of Instruction

English is the language of instruction in most community colleges outside Quebec, but French language instruction is available in many programs and in most regions. New Brunswick's college system includes both English and French campuses; Ontario has three French-language colleges; and a number of bilingual institutions, like Ontario's Cambrian College, offer programs in both languages. Manitoba's École technique et professionnelle at the Collège universitaire de Saint-Boniface serves francophone students in that province.

Tuition Fees

Community college tuition fees vary, but are lower than university fees in every province. Post-secondary college students are eligible for the same government financial assistance programs as university students (see page 59 and 74).

Although residences are often available for out-of-town students, community colleges draw most of their students from the local area. As a result, college students often avoid many of the living costs associated with university study.

Community College Governance

Canadian community colleges are neither autonomous institutions nor extensions of provincial departments. Like universities, most are governed by a board of governors, either appointed by the provincial or municipal government, or elected. But their boards do not enjoy the same level of autonomy that characterizes university governance. Because colleges have become important instruments of labour market and job development policy, provincial governments are more directly involved in their admission policies, curriculum, planning and working conditions.

To help ensure that their programs are relevant and responsive to employer needs in the community or region, colleges also rely on advisory councils to strengthen their links with business and industry. These councils, which include representatives from industry, labour unions, and college instructional staff, assist colleges in developing courses, changing course content to reflect new developments, and evaluating program success.[36] In most jurisdictions, advisory councils report to the board of governors.

One province has an executive body to deal specifically with community colleges. Ontario's Council of Regents for the Colleges of Applied Arts and Technology appoints governors to college boards, conducts collective agreement negotiations (as the employer) for the colleges, and advises the Minister of Education and Training on system-wide issues.

Focus on Student Learning

Colleges typically provide a more job-related curriculum than universities, featuring smaller classes, off-campus course delivery, a greater ratio of laboratory space to classroom space, a more interactive teaching style and more inclusive entry criteria. [37]

Canada's community colleges consider themselves primarily teaching institutions, and place their highest priority on effective teaching environments and techniques. Their teachers come from a variety of backgrounds: business, industry, trades, social services, universities and public education. Many bring extensive industry-based experience to their jobs, or hold advanced degrees or doctorates in their disciplines. Since research and institutional governance are not usually considered part of the job for college teachers, faculty members spend most of their time in classrooms, and in direct contact with students.

---

[36] *The Directory of Canadian Colleges and Institutes* (Ottawa: ACCC, 1992), p. viii.
[37] ACCC, *Getting to Know Us, op. cit.*

Some Highlights of Canadian Post-secondary Education

Co-operative Education

Canadian colleges and universities have been pioneers in co-operative education. Co-op integrates academic studies with job placements relating to the student's field of study by alternating periods of employment with periods of study. It gives students an opportunity to "test the waters" in their chosen fields, to apply classroom theory in the workplace, and to learn about the expectations of employers. Since co-op students are paid competitive wages for the work they do, they can earn a significant portion of their post-secondary expenses during their work terms. As an added benefit, many students find full-time employment with their co-op employers after graduation.

Co-op education has become popular with employers, as well. It gives them an opportunity to hire young people to meet short-term or just-in-time labour requirements, to provide input into relevant curriculum, and to pre-screen potential employees. Employers can choose from a pool of nearly 56,000 (1996) college and university students in computer science, engineering, business, communications, electronics, the arts, sciences and trades.[38]

In 1978-79, only 21 institutes, colleges and universities offered co-operative education programs; by 1994/95 co-op was available at 129 institutions in every province and territory. Programs are most available, and enrolments are highest, in Ontario, Quebec and British Columbia.[39]

Distance Education

Given its size and sparse population, it is not surprising that Canada has become a world leader in distance education. In 1994, 54% of universities and 68% of colleges delivered some programs via distance education.[40] Statistics Canada reports that 7% of adult educa-

---

[38] *1995-1996 National Co-operative Education Directory* (Toronto: Canadian Association for Co-operative Education/Association canadienne de l'enseignement coopératif, 1996), p. vi.

[39] *Ibid.*, pp. xix - xxi.

[40] CMEC, *Development of Education, op. cit.*, p. 44.

tion — 10% in rural areas — is delivered through distance education. (These numbers include students at all levels.)[41]

Opportunities to pursue post-secondary degrees and diplomas via distance education exist nation-wide. In three provinces, non-campus universities serve distance students exclusively: Open Learning Institute in British Columbia, Athabasca University in Alberta, and Télé-université in Quebec, the only French-language university in North America specializing in distance education. Manitoba's three universities offer courses via distance education to remote northern communities. Ontario provides distance education through Contact North, a communication network which delivers almost 600 secondary, college and university courses to 100 Northern Ontario communities, and also operates Collège des Grands Lacs, a college of applied arts and technology in southern Ontario. All of New Brunswick's universities have distance education programs, as do Nova Scotia's Community College and Collège de l'Acadie, and Memorial University of Newfoundland and Labrador. Since 1991, Television Northern Canada (TVNC) has been providing post-secondary educational programming to northern Canada, involving Yukon College and Newfoundland's Community College campus in Labrador.

Distance education still relies heavily on print, audio cassettes, videotapes and televised courses, but these are rapidly being augmented by more interactive methods like audioconferencing, videoconferencing and computer-assisted courses. However, developments on the Internet may outpace all other developments. Simon Fraser University in British Columbia has launched an experimental "Virtual University" to connect 750 students and 130 professors at 12 test sites, including the University of Alberta and Université Laval in Quebec.[42] The project, which has received funds from both the federal government and industry, represents only the tip of the iceberg as educators use the Internet to cross institutional and geographic barriers.

Some distance educators sound a note of caution, however. Although more and more homes are equipped with a computer and a modem, the technology is not yet as universal as telephones and televisions. Until it is, equity will continue to be an issue when designing distance education programs based on the Internet.

---

[41] Rachel Bernier, "Distance Learning: An Idea Whose Time Has Come," *Education Quarterly Review* 2:3 (1995), p. 40.

[42] "A Crash Course in Reality 101," *op. cit.*, p. 53.

Post-secondary Education:
An International Dimension

Canadian post-secondary institutions attract students from around the world. In 1992, Canada ranked fifth in the world in the number of international post-secondary students it hosted — behind the United States, France, Germany and the United Kingdom. In 1994, 65,000 international students attended Canada's colleges and universities, 25,500 at the college level (27.5%), 22,900 at the university undergraduate level (24.7%), and 16,600 (17.9%) at the graduate level. It should be noted that the Statistics Canada figures include only full-time students at the college/trade level. They account for only a small percentage (roughly one-sixth) of the "student authorizations" granted by Citizenship and Immigration Canada, suggesting that a large number of international students at the college level are studying part-time, and have work permits as well.[43]

The international student population enriches the learning environment on Canadian campuses, and at the same time brings significant revenues to institutions at a time when their budgets are under pressure. In most provinces, foreign students pay higher fees than Canadian students, as shown in the chart on page 60, although in some provinces the universities do not keep the differenital revenue.

In 1993-94, the vast majority of international students attended colleges and universities in the four largest provinces: 48% in Ontario, 17% in British Columbia; 16% in Quebec; and 8% in Alberta. Although they represented more than 200 countries, the majority came from Asia, particularly east Asia. Europe, the United States, and Central America send significant numbers of students to Canada, as well.

Full-time international students are more likely to be enrolled in universities than in colleges, with a high proportion in sciences and graduate programs. The University of Toronto, McGill University, the Université de Montréal, and the University of British Columbia accept the largest number of international students.[44]

Universities set their own requirements for international students, and assess their prior qualifications individually. As a rule, they must meet the university's admission standards and, if their native language is not English or French, demonstrate an ability to study in

---

[43] Tina Chui, "International Students in Canada," *Education Quarterly Review* 3:3 (1996), pp. 42-44; and *International Student Participation in Canadian Education 1992* (Ottawa: Statistics Canada, 1994), Cat. 81-261, pp. 17, 25.

[44] Tina Chui, *op. cit.*, pp. 43-44.

one of Canada's official languages. This usually means scoring 550 or better on the Test of English as a Foreign Language (TOEFL) or the equivalent French test.[45] The Canadian Information Centre for International Credentials (CICIC) acts as a national clearinghouse for Canadian and international educational credentials.[46]

Foreign students interested in Canadian colleges or universities must apply for and obtain a student visa, which will allow them to reside in Canada for the purposes of education. It will not, under normal circumstances, allow them to take employment.

Colleges and universities are involved in a wide range of activities and programs aimed at improving international co-operation. These include student and faculty exchanges, joint research projects, and international development projects.

Paying for Post-secondary Education

Like elementary and secondary education, post-secondary education is formally under the jurisdiction of the provinces and territories. In most provinces, a single department shares responsibility for elementary, secondary and post-secondary education. Unlike public schools, however, universities and colleges receive some direct support — and substantial indirect support — from the federal government. Its transfer grants and tax points cover approximately half the cost of post-secondary education, its student loan program supplements provincial funds to make post-secondary education accessible to most eligible Canadians, and many of its departments direct some support to relevant post-secondary programs.

Of the $57.1 billion spent on education in Canada in 1994-95, 27% ($15.9 billion) was spent on post-secondary education, and 10% ($6 billion) on training.[47] This amount includes both expenditures by post-secondary institutions themselves and expenditures by governments on scholarships and student aid.

Federal and provincial governments continue to foot most of the post-secondary bill, but the contribution from student fees is growing.

---

[45] "Canadian Higher Education", *op. cit.*, p. viii.
[46] CMEC, *The Development of Education, op. cit.*, p. 41.
[47] Stephen Lawton, *op. cit.*, p. 162.

The following chart of 1995-96 expenditures shows the break-down of revenues to post-secondary institutions and programs, with federal and provincial governments contributing 74%; student tuitions, 14%; and other sources (private donations and bequests, investment income, and sale of services), 12%.

**Expenditure on Post-secondary Education
by Direct Source of Funds, 1995-96**

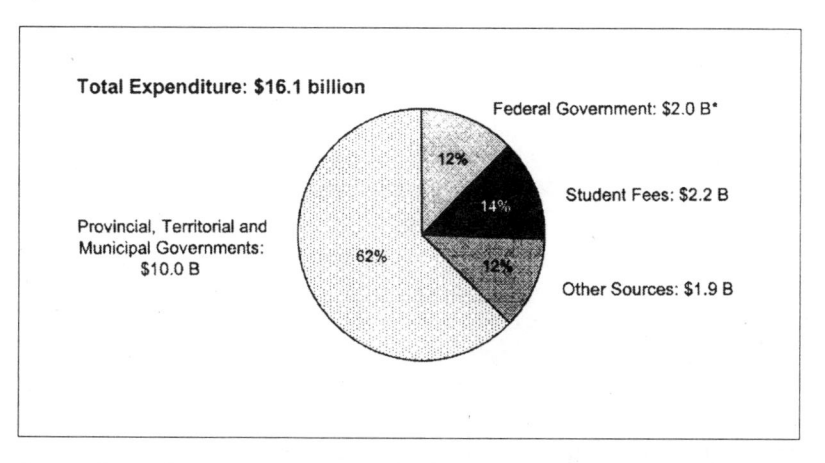

- Total Expenditure: $16.1 billion
- Federal Government: $2.0 B*
- Student Fees: $2.2 B
- Other Sources: $1.9 B
- Provincial, Territorial and Municipal Governments: $10.0 B (62%)
- 12%, 14%, 12%

Source: Human Resources Development Canada, *Federal and Provincial Support to Post-secondary Education in Canada: A Report to Parliament 1995-96* (Ottawa: Supply and Services Canada, 1997), p. 4.

Note: *Since the chart identifies expenditures by direct source of funds, federal contributions to provincial/territorial governments are not identified. In 1995-96, these contributions included $6.3 billion under EPF transfers and $67.0 million under the post-secondary component of the Official Languages in Education Program.

Institutional Funding

In keeping with the constitutional delegation of responsibility, provincial and territorial governments are the primary source of direct funding for the operation of Canada's universities and colleges. They use a variety of mechanisms to allocate provincial funds to colleges and universities, including block funding based on budgets or audited statements, enrolment-driven grant formulas, and program-based funding.

Much of this provincial money actually originates in the coffers of the federal government. Between 1977 and 1995, Established Programs Financing (EPF) provided the provinces with federal funds targeted for post-secondary education, based on a per capita formula — a total of $6.2 billion in 1994-95. In 1996, a new Canada Health and Social Transfer (CHST) replaced the EPF and the Canada Assistance Plan. The new program continues to transfer federal funds to the provinces, but leaves the allocation between education and social services to the discretion of the provincial governments. The introduction of the CHST was accompanied by significant reductions in total transfers as part of the federal government's deficit reduction efforts.[48]

Transfer payments are supplementary to a national equalization program which helps poorer provinces maintain public services without imposing an undue burden of provincial taxation. Equalization payments flow to the governments of the Atlantic Provinces, Quebec, Manitoba and Saskatchewan, which can apply the funds to any program area.[49]

All federal departments provide some support to post-secondary education through programs that support their own objectives. For example, Industry Canada supports science, engineering and technology students through its Canada Scholarship Program; Health Canada makes contributions toward university research through the National Health Research and Development Program; Canadian Heritage supports minority-language education through the Official Languages in Education Program; and Environment Canada funds fellowships, research chairs and grants within the social and natural sciences, engineering and health sciences. The federal government also provides support for university research through the Natural Sciences and Engineering Research Council, the Medical Research Council, the Social Sciences and Humanities Research Council, and the National Research Council.

Student Loans

Provinces and territories, as well as the federal government, make a further contribution to post-secondary education through their student support programs, which are intended to ensure that all qualified students can afford a post-secondary education. Financial assistance is available through a combination of the federally funded Canada Student Loans Program (CSLP) and the provinces' own

---
[48] HRDC, *op. cit.*, p. 21.
[49] *Ibid.*, p. 3-4.

programs of loans, grants and scholarships. Quebec and the Northwest Territories do not participate in the CSLP, and so receive alternative payments from the federal government to operate their own programs. The provinces and territories determine the details of eligibility and levels of support, but organizations representing governments and the post-secondary education community meet regularly to co-ordinate their policies.

Canada student loans are available to full-time and part-time students, as a supplement to resources available from family contributions, scholarships, and their own employment earnings. The federal government pays interest on student loans as long as students are in full-time study; part-time students pay interest on their loans while in school.

Because rising tuition rates are resulting in higher debt levels for many students, the federal government is developing a strategy for managing student debt, including new grant programs for students with special needs, Youth Service Canada completion vouchers, and expanded interest relief for low-income workers. The government is exploring options relating to partial loan forgiveness and more flexible repayment options. Interest in an income contingent loan repayment plan has been growing at all levels of government.[50]

Tax Supports for Post-secondary Education

In addition to transferring funds directly to provinces, institutions or students, governments also support post-secondary education with tax deductions and exemptions. These include tax credits for charitable contributions to educational institutions, for full-time post-secondary students, and for tuition fees; tax exemptions for the first $500 of scholarship income; and special tax benefits for Registered Education Savings Plans. Universities and colleges are also eligible for a 67% rebate on the Goods and Services Tax (GST) paid on taxable purchases, and many are exempt from provincial and/or municipal property taxes.

---

[50] *Ibid.*, pp. 21-22; and CMEC, *Development of Education, op. cit.*, p. 40.

Chapter 3

LIFELONG LEARNING: ADULT EDUCATION IN CANADA

Education for Employment

> *More and better learning means more and better jobs. Countless studies confirm this connection between a highly skilled workforce and a high-wage economy. How well people live...depends on how well they learn.*[1]

Trade/Vocational and Preparatory Programs

FOR MANY YOUNG ADULTS, trade and vocational training follows immediately after secondary school, and serves as a third formal post-secondary option. Unlike university and college, however, these programs do not require a secondary school diploma.

Trade and vocational training prepares students to be job-ready in specific skill areas, combining classroom study with on-the-job training. With the exception of apprenticeship programs, training courses are usually of one year's duration or less, and sometimes as short as a few weeks. They include pre-employment or pre-apprenticeship programs, registered apprenticeship programs, skills-upgrading, and other short-term training in practical

---

[1] *Learning Well....Living Well* (Ottawa: Prosperity Secretariat, Supply and Services Canada, 1991), p. vi.

skills that can be applied immediately in the labour market. Employers and labour unions frequently design courses focusing on very specific skills that are in immediate demand.

Preparatory training upgrades skill levels to a point where students can benefit from further vocational training or post-secondary education. It includes pre-vocational academic upgrading, language training, job readiness training, and orientation programs.

Community colleges are Canada's primary providers of both training and preparatory programs. In 1990-91, trade and vocational training accounted for nearly one quarter of college teaching activity, and preparatory training for 8%.[2] To a lesser extent, private and commercial schools, universities and school boards also provide training. Nova Scotia, New Brunswick, Quebec, Manitoba, Saskatchewan, Alberta, and British Columbia have specialized vocational schools, including government training schools, vocational training centres and other specialized training institutions.

Demographics and employment levels influence the demand for both trade/vocational and preparatory training. When employment opportunities are limited, many people turn to specialized training and skills upgrading to improve their job prospects, and governments are more likely to provide assistance to train or retrain individuals for trades that are experiencing labour shortages. In 1990-91, 167,000 Canadians were enrolled in trade and vocational programs — a sharp decline from the recession of a few years earlier, suggesting that, as jobs became more readily available, demand for training decreased. Pre-apprenticeship training experienced the greatest decline, due in part to a steady drop in the youth population during the 1980s. Preparatory programs, which are particularly useful in helping people enter the workforce during a period of expansion, increased slightly in the late 1980s, reaching 95,907 in 1990-91.[3]

In keeping with their traditional dominance in the trades, men continued to outnumber women in trade and vocational programs by almost three to one, although targeted government programs to help train and employ women in the trades succeeded in increasing their participation rate slightly. On the other hand, preparatory programs attracted a majority of women, many of whom were seeking entry-

---

[2] Stephen B. Lawton, *Financing Canadian Education* (Toronto: Canadian Education Association, 1996), p. 173.

[3] Karl Skof, "Enrolment Changes in Trade/Vocational and Preparatory Programs, 1983-84 to 1990-91," *Education Quarterly Review, 1994*, vol. 1, no. 1 (Ottawa: Statistics Canada, 1994), p. 35-38.

Lifelong Learning

level qualifications for the job market or prerequisite skills for further training.[4]

Although provincial governments often include training in their education portfolios, it is not as limited to the provincial domain as elementary, secondary, and post-secondary education. The federal government supports training activities through both consolidated revenue funds and employment insurance funds dedicated to assisting unemployed Canadians. The provinces make their own financial contributions to training and provide incentives to support on-the-job training. They tend to focus on preparatory academic programs, language instruction in English and French, continuing education, and pre-employment readiness training.[5]

Ottawa's substantial commitment to training hinges on its responsibility for income support programs. "The federal government's obligation for employment insurance and welfare payments makes it doubly interested in training: when successful, the newly trained individual moves into employment, saving the government direct expenditures and generating new tax revenue."[6] Since the mid-1980s, the federal government's Labour Force Development Strategy has shifted emphasis away from the purchase of service from institutions and toward private sector trainers.

Despite the federal government's current involvement in training programs, their future may be in the hands of the provinces. In the current process of decentralizing government, manpower training is likely to become an exclusive provincial responsibility. This shift may lead to less consistent training opportunities nationally, since not all provinces make the same commitment to training programs.

Apprenticeship Training

Apprenticeship programs combine classroom instruction, taken at a designated community college or similar institution, with on-the-job training under a journeyman's supervision (except in Quebec, where they consist only of on-the-job training). Provincial and territorial departments of labour or manpower set standards and qualifications for registered apprentices; non-registered apprentices can enter into private agreements with employers, sometimes in association

---

[4] *Ibid.*, p. 40-41.
[5] Stephen Lawton, *op. cit.*, p. 174.
[6] *Ibid.*, p. 172.

with a labour union. Standard interprovincial examinations ensure a measure of consistency in training and promote the mobility of journeymen within Canada.

Apprentices can expect to spend four or five years working under a journeyman before achieving journeyman status, themselves. During that time they are paid relatively low apprenticeship wages, which vary according to the trade.

Apprenticeship training has long been one of the weakest links in Canada's education and training system. High school vocational programs leading to apprenticeship attract only 10% of secondary students. The links between secondary schools and apprenticeship programs are uneven and incomplete, as reflected in the average age of Canadian apprentices. At 26, they are nearly 10 years older than their German counterparts, having turned to apprenticeship after several years of disappointment in the job market.[7]

Although the labour market has changed dramatically in the past two decades, Canada's apprenticeship programs have not changed to meet it. The system is still largely concentrated in the manufacturing and construction trades, and in traditional service occupations like baking and hairdressing, even though the majority of new jobs are now in new technologies and new service sectors.

A number of provinces have undertaken initiatives to strengthen the apprenticeship program for students who wish to pursue employment in the skilled trades.

The Canadian Labour Force Development Board

The Canadian Labour Force Development Board (CLFDB) was established in 1991 as a national, not-for-profit organization designed to give labour and business a greater role in training and human resource development. Its mandate is to lead in developing a commitment to training and labour force development in Canada; to advocate for relevant, high quality, and accessible training; to provide direction on key aspects of training and labour adjustment policies and programs; and to give labour market partners an opportunity to work together.[8]

---

[7] *A Lot to Learn: Education and Training in Canada: A Summary* (Ottawa: Economic Council of Canada, 1992), pp. 13, 16.

[8] "What is the CLFDB?" (http://www.magi.com/~clfdb/indexhtml#clfdb) 11 April 1997.

The board works in collaboration with more than 20 industry-led sector councils. These were organized as a federal initiative to encourage business and labour to co-operate in building a training culture and to take joint responsibility for identifying training needs and establishing programs. The councils represent business and labour from major sectors of the Canadian economy (for example, the Canadian Automotive Repair and Service Council, the Canadian Council of Professional Engineers, the Canadian Council for Human Resources in the Environment Industry, and the National Seafood Sector Council).

In addition to bringing labour and management from various industrial sectors together, the CLFDB has given Canada's educators and trainers an opportunity to work together in a national forum with their primary constituents. In doing so, they were struck by the need for greater co-ordination among training providers — whether community colleges, universities, community-based trainers or volunteers. In 1997, a report of the Education/Training Provider Network Project proposed that trainers from across Canada explore opportunities for co-operation and collaboration, including the development of a Provider Network Corporation to serve as a national clearinghouse for training programs.

Creating a Learning Culture

> *What was once a 'front-end' education system where most people prepared for a job in the first two decades of life is now becoming a system where learning never stops."*[9]

Adult Continuing Education

The changing economy has made Canada a nation of learners. One in every four adult Canadians is enrolled in some form of

---

[9] *Lifelong Learning and the New Economy: Summary Report* (Toronto: The Premier's Council on Economic Renewal, 1995), p. 2.

Lifelong Learning

educational program to improve basic academic skills, acquire or upgrade specific job skills, prepare for new employment opportunities, increase general knowledge, or pursue personal interests. As the workforce becomes more mobile and long-term job security becomes a thing of the past for many workers, Canadians are adapting to changing requirements by learning new skills in record numbers. In 1993, 5.8 million adult Canadians (28%) engaged in education and training activities outside the regular school or university systems, a 6% increase over 1991. In the primary working years (age 25-44) the participation rate reached 35%.[10] These statistics support the conventional wisdom that the new economy is turning Canadians into lifelong learners who can expect to acquire new skills throughout their lives in order to remain competitive in their existing jobs or retrain for new ones.

Although most adult learners study to further their careers, a significant minority enrols in courses for personal interest only.

Participation in adult education is not evenly distributed across

The Learning Continuum

Source: *A Lot to Learn: Education and Training in Canada, A Summary* (Ottawa: Economic Council of Canada, 1992), p. 12.

---

[10] L. Shipley, "An Overview of Adult Education and Training in Canada," *1994 Adult Education and Training Survey* (Ottawa: HRDC and Statistics Canada, 1997), pp. 9, 11.

Canada, ranging in 1993 from a low of 19% in Newfoundland to a high of 35% in British Columbia. Participation rates gradually increase from the Atlantic region, through Central Canada and the Prairies, to the West Coast. A number of factors may contribute to this variation, including the level of employment, the general economic well being of the region, the industrial structure of the province, and the availability of resources for education and training.[11] In addition to regional variation, participation rates also vary according to previous educational attainment, employment status, income, occupational level, and employer. As a rule, the best educated workers, who are relatively well positioned within their places of employment, are most likely to benefit from further education and training.

The Role of Educational Institutions

Outside formal post-secondary programs, no organization or type of institution has a monopoly on educational programs for adults. Until recently, most continuing education programs were offered on the fringes of the Canadian education system, run by non-professionals and volunteers. Although it is not as well funded as post-secondary education, continuing education is now firmly established in publicly funded institutions. Schools, colleges and universities have become the primary providers of adult education and training activities, accounting for one-third of all training programs. They are followed by employers and commercial suppliers, who provide approximately one-fifth each.[12]

Community colleges play the primary institutional role in delivering adult continuing education. In their summary of the community colleges' role, Dennison and Gallagher give a snapshot of the kinds of programs available to adult learners outside the formal post-secondary degree, diploma and certificate programs:

- vocational and trades training programs of different but usually short durations, intended to lead directly to employment;
- apprenticeship training programs;
- general programs of an academic, rather than job training, nature;
- personal interest and community development programs;
- pre-college level or upgrading programs, or basic skill training;

---

[11] L. Shipley, *op. cit.*, p. 10.
[12] "Highlights," *1994 Adult Education and Training Survey* (Ottawa: HRDC and Statistics Canada, 1997), p. 2.

- contracted programs, supplying training to corporations, community agencies and government departments.[13]

Universities also offer non-credit continuing education courses as part of their mandate to provide greater public access to university services, and to respond to community needs. A growing number of university continuing education courses are funded through contracts with government, associations or businesses.

Local school boards often offer continuing education courses in the evenings. In some provinces government funding supports these programs; in others school boards must operate them on a cost-recovery basis. Even when provincial funding is not available for general interest courses, special grants often provide support for academic upgrading and literacy programs. Typical school board continuing education programs include English or French as a second language, computer technology, and special interest subjects related to job skills and personal interests.

Half of all education and training activities were concentrated in three areas of study in 1993: Commerce, Management and Business Administration; Engineering/Applied Sciences Technologies and Trades; and Health Professions, Sciences and Technologies.[14] In university continuing education, the most popular courses are business, followed by English, computer science, and liberal arts.[15]

For the minority (less than 10%) of adult learners enrolled in a formal educational program, only school boards, community colleges, and universities can offer credit courses toward a diploma, certificate, or degree. But most adults are not interested in obtaining formal credentials; they sign up for individual courses based on immediate need or interest. They choose from a wide range of non-credit courses within the continuing education departments of educational institutions, at their local community or sports centre, through their union or professional association, or with a private instructor. Younger adults are more likely to turn to educational institutions for their continuing education, while older adults rely more heavily on their employers.

Since post-secondary institutions, business colleges, and private training schools are concentrated in cities, urban Canadians can

---

[13] John D. Dennison and Paul Gallagher, *Canada's Community Colleges: A Critical Analysis* (Vancouver: University of British Columbia Press, 1986), pp. 70-72.
[14] "Highlights," *1994 Adult Education and Training in Canada, op. cit.*, p. 2.
[15] Statistics Canada, *The Daily*, 7 April 1997 (11-001E).

Lifelong Learning

choose from many more continuing education options than rural Canadians. In fact, participation in rural communities and remote areas is about 5% lower than in cities.[16] Distance education and new communication technologies are playing a growing role in closing that gap; provincially supported educational television services carry both formal and non-formal study units, and many institutions offer continuing education programs via correspondence. At the same time, computer technologies are making self-instruction more available and more effective. (See page 69 for a discussion of distance education.)

The Role of Employers

Since 71% of adult learners are engaged in programs to improve their job skills, and 70% of those are sponsored in full or in part by their employers, employers have a major influence on the distribution of adult education and training opportunities. In 1993, one in every five persons in the workforce had some education and training sponsored by the employer.[17]

A 1994 Statistics Canada study found that the rate of participation in job-related education/training increased steadily among employees until about age 40. The same study found that more than 45% of university graduates in the 30-34 age group participated in some form of work-related education, compared to 30% for the age group as a whole, suggesting that employers tend to concentrate their education and training efforts on those employees who already have the highest education levels.[18]

Employer support for education and training takes a variety of forms: paid time off, paid tuition fees, and provision of course materials are the most popular. Large firms are much more likely to provide training for their employees than smaller firms. Although large companies represent only 1% of employment, they accounted for 45% of all training expenditures in 1987. Most small firms provide some training to their employees, but only 27% conduct formal training, compared to 76% of large corporations.[19] Larger employers are more likely to deliver their own training programs; smaller firms are more likely to contract with external consultants.

Employment-based training appears to perpetuate itself. Individuals with high levels of education and training are most likely to

---

[16] L. Shipley, *op. cit.*, p. 11.
[17] "Highlights," *op. cit.*, p. 2.
[18] Canadian Education Statistics Council, *Indicators, op. cit.*, p. 90.
[19] *A Lot to Learn, op. cit.*, p. 17.

feel the need for even more. Of the total population age 17 and over, only 8% claim to have unsatisfied training needs; that proportion jumps to more than one in three among those who have already received some education or training with the assistance of their employer. "It seems, therefore, that the more training people receive or the higher their level of education, the more they are aware of the value and relevance of training to working effectively — and the more training they are likely to request."[20]

The Role of Governments

Although both federal and provincial governments provide some support for adult education, it does not fall within their mandates as clearly as elementary, secondary, and post-secondary education, or trade and vocational training. When government funding is not available, continuing education programs operate on a cost-recovery basis, with fees paid by students or employers. The 1992 Adult Education and Training Survey notes that adult education and training is the four-way responsibility of individuals, who identify their education and training needs; employers, who encourage the education and training of their employees; institutions, which respond to the needs of adult learners; and governments, which are responsible for ensuring access to education and mobility of learners.[21]

The issue of access was raised by Statistics Canada in its *1992 Adult Education and Training Survey*, and echoed by statistics from its 1994 survey. In reporting that adults with low incomes and less education have greater difficulty obtaining the education and training they require, it warned of the "very real risk of the development of two polarized populations in terms of access to adult education and training."[22]

Literacy Programs

Adult literacy received wide public attention in Canada when the Southam Literacy Survey was released in 1986. That survey found more than one in every five Canadian-born adults, aged 18 and over, to be functionally illiterate in English or French. Its figures were borne

---
[20] CESC, *Indicators, op. cit.*, p. 94.
[21] *1992 Adult Education and Training in Canada* (Ottawa: HRDC and Statistics Canada, 1995), p. 78.
[22] *Ibid.*, p. 77.

out by a Statistics Canada survey three years later, which found that the reading skills of 16% of adults were too limited for them to deal with most of the written material encountered in everyday life. An additional 22% could carry out simple reading tasks, but lacked the skills to cope with more complex written material.

Literacy programs do not fall under the clear mandate of any single government or agency. They are offered in the community, based on demand, by school boards, community colleges, private institutions, and local organizations, many of which rely on volunteers. They receive support from both federal and provincial sources, but funding is frequently project-based, making it difficult for literacy programs and organizations to achieve long-term stability.

In 1987, the federal government established the National Literacy Secretariat (NLS) to support the literacy effort. Through federal-provincial joint funding arrangements, NLS sponsors literacy projects that are directed to regional or local needs. It also funds national projects in partnership with a variety of non-governmental and voluntary organizations, including literacy groups and business and labour organizations.

The National Adult Literacy Database Inc. (NALD) is a non-profit service organization that provides a single-source database of adult literacy programs, resources, services and activities for teachers, volunteers, program administrators, policy-setters and learners. NALD, based in Fredericton, New Brunswick, is funded by the National Literacy Secretariat of Human Resource Development Canada, and supported by the Government of New Brunswick, Ontario's Fanshawe College of Applied Arts and Technology, the Movement for Canadian Literacy, the Association of Canadian Community Colleges, and ABC Canada (a national literacy organization).

Adult Education: Changing Perspectives

Most Canadians still think of education as a series of formal programs leading to a life of employment. The reality is quite different. As the 20th century comes to a close, there are almost as many adults enrolled in education and training activities as there are students in regular full-time school programs in Canada.[23] Changes in the workforce are creating a demand for adult learning which presents a challenge to both governments and institutions.

---

[23] *Ibid.*

Lifelong Learning

Governments are beginning to recognize the importance of lifelong education and training as a prerequisite to economic success in the global economy, and to the societal well being that accompanies a productive workforce. In 1991, the federal government's Prosperity Secretariat's *Learning Well...Living Well* called on Canadians to focus their attention on the development of a learning culture. Since that time, the provinces have been engaged in massive educational reform. In the process, some are introducing changes to meet the growing demand for lifelong learning. Ontario's Task Force on Lifelong Learning, which issued its report, *Lifelong Learning and the New Economy* in 1995, referred to lifelong learning as "a foundation for the province's economic renewal;"[24] Alberta's *New Directions for Adult Learning in Alberta* (1994) proposed a "roadmap" for meeting the demands for "greater employability and personal growth through opportunities to learn;"[25] British Columbia's *Charting a New Course* (1996) proposed a mission for post-secondary education and training that acknowledges the importance of lifelong learning in providing adults with "flexible learning opportunities throughout their lives."[26]

The growing importance of adult education in the late 20th century echoes the boom in post-secondary education during the 1960s and 1970s. At that time, the economy was in overdrive, and the population bulge created by the post-war baby boom was poised to enter Canada's universities and colleges. Post-secondary education rose rapidly to the top of the public agenda. That generation is now in mid-career, facing a constricting economy and an increasingly competitive workplace. Its demands for continuing education and training are reinforced by Canada's need to improve its competitive advantage in the global economy. In the climate of the late 1990s, these demands are unlikely to be met by governments alone. Instead, they are being met by new partnerships among business, labour, government, and public institutions. Their challenge will be to ensure that those partnerships create a lifelong learning culture that reaches into all sectors of society and the workforce.

---

[24] "Message from the Deputy Minister," *Lifelong Learning and the New Economy, op. cit.*, p. i.

[25] *New Directions for Adult Learning in Alberta* (Edmonton: Alberta Advanced Education and Career Development, 1994), p. 2.

[26] *Charting a New Course: A Strategic Plan For the Future of British Columbia's College, Institute and Agency System* (Victoria, BC: Ministry of Education, Skills and Training, 1996), p. 7.

Chapter 4

EDUCATIONAL TRENDS IN CANADA

EDUCATION IN CANADA is constantly changing to reflect new economic, social, and political realities. In its introduction to *Education Initiatives in Canada, 1996*, the Council of Ministers of Education, Canada (CMEC) identified a number of key trends that are consistent across Canada. In elementary and secondary education, the ministers noted an increased emphasis on curriculum outcomes and standards, more testing and provincial examinations, acceptance of information technology as an integral part of education, and a new focus on transition programs designed to help students move from school to the world of work.[1]

Greater Emphasis on Curriculum Outcomes and Assessment

For the past decade or more, the Canadian public has been demanding greater accountability for student outcomes. A 1993 public opinion poll by the Angus Reid Group found that Canadians overwhelmingly supported a "back to the basics" approach to teaching the fundamentals of literacy and numeracy. It also found, however, that the public had broadened its definition of the basics to include an emphasis on skills training in secondary school and on technology at all levels.[2]

Although the basics were never abandoned in Canadian schools, many felt that they had been diluted by a barrage of new curricular demands on teachers, and by methodologies that allowed students to learn at their own pace in less structured classroom environments.

---

[1] *Education Initiatives in Canada, 1996: A Report from the Provinces and Territories* (Toronto: CMEC, 1996), p. ii.

[2] Angus Reid Group, "A National Survey of Public Opinion and Attitudes: Education Issues Confronting Canada," *CEA Newsletter*, October-November 1993, p. 5.

Educational Trends

Post-secondary institutions and employers expressed dismay at the level of preparedness they were finding in high school graduates. At the same time, Canada's performance on international tests of literacy, numeracy and science skills received considerable media attention, and raised public concern that Canadian students were failing to keep up with those in other industrialized nations. Parent groups have formed at the local, provincial, and national levels to lobby for a renewed emphasis on basic skills, teacher-centred instruction, and stricter evaluation measures.

As a result of these concerns, most provinces have been revising their curricula to place a greater emphasis on the core subject areas of reading, mathematics, and science, and to reduce the number of optional credits in secondary school. Educators continue to recognize that all children do not learn at the same pace, but they are returning to more objective criteria and expectations, and more traditional teaching methods. New core curricula in most provinces are specifying expected outcomes for age and grade levels and incorporating regular evaluation of those outcomes into the school program. Some provinces are moving away from the recent practice of moving children from grade to grade with their peers, regardless of achievement level.

The new emphasis on standardized outcomes and core subjects is reflected in the development of regional and national guidelines and standards. In 1993 the Atlantic provinces endorsed the development of a regional curriculum, with flexibility to accommodate significant differences among provinces. In the same year, the four western provinces and two territories signed the Western Canadian Protocol for Collaboration in Basic Education. At the national level, the CMEC has spearheaded a project, involving all provinces except Quebec, to develop a science curriculum framework for kindergarten to grade 12. In addition to promoting an efficient use of resources, regional curriculum frameworks ensure that students acquire the same essential knowledge and skills and can move freely from one province to another without encountering gaps in their schooling.

More objective performance criteria lead naturally to an emphasis on testing and evaluation. In addition to increasing testing at the classroom level, most provinces have introduced a provincial assessment program to evaluate system-wide performance. High school exit exams for graduating students, which were unpopular in the 1970s and 1980s, are now required in nine provinces.[3] The CMEC's School Achievement Indicators Program tests mathematics, reading, writing

---
[3] OECD, *Education at a Glance, op. cit.*, p. 262.

Educational Trends

and science across the country on a rotating basis.

New concerns about student achievement have also been accompanied by a renewed interest in teacher education, both pre-service and in-service. Many provinces have been reviewing their teacher education programs to prepare teachers for new expectations; some, like Nova Scotia, are considering regular recertification to ensure that teachers remain up-to-date.

The Technology Revolution in the Classroom

Technology itself is not new, but its importance as an educational issue has exploded in the past few years as computers have moved into classrooms and workplaces. No longer simply an object of study for those who wish to pursue "technical" careers, technology — particularly computer technology — has become an essential educational tool. Like reading or writing, it is now recognized as a prerequisite for student success. Word processing, simulations, and computerized data analysis have become as standard in schools as typewriters and adding machines a generation ago. In fact, the technological revolution is moving at such a rapid pace that any review of "current" activities is certain to be obsolete by the time it is read.

Canada was one of the first countries in the world to link its entire student body to the information highway. In 1995 Newfoundland became the first province with full Internet access, linking all schools to the World Wide Web and the Internet; by 1997, virtually all schools in the country had access to the Internet via the SchoolNet national electronic network. Despite overall reductions in education budgets, most provinces have introduced systematic plans to expand the role of technology in curriculum, primarily through the acquisition of computer hardware and software for classroom use.

A number of provinces have set specific targets for classroom computer acquisition. For example, British Columbia announced a five-year plan in 1995 to have one computer in place for every three secondary students and every six elementary students, and Nova Scotia has set a goal of one computer for every ten students by the year 2000. To help the provinces meet these objectives, Industry Canada's "Computers in the Schools" program has moved thousands of used computers, software and other technologies from industry into Canadian classrooms. In co-operation with provincial and territorial governments and the private sector, the program had placed more than 20,000 computers and 40,000 pieces of software in schools and libraries by 1997.

Educational Trends

Once in place, computers are being used to train teachers as well as students, and to offer computer training and Internet access to the community. Human Resources Development Canada has set up the Office of Learning Technologies (OLT) expressly to provide funding support to innovative learning opportunities using new technologies.

Proponents of computers in schools see them as a powerful tool for levelling the playing field in Canadian classrooms. Their capacity to retrieve information is nearly limitless, and equally available in urban, rural and remote locations; they can be equipped with features that allow many children with disabilities to work alongside their classmates; and they increase understanding within Canada and internationally by allowing students to connect with individuals and classrooms across the country and around the world.

Nevertheless, there are those who have reservations about the expanding role of computer technology in schools. Some parents and teachers continue to fear that, in the face of reduced school budgets, students may find themselves facing machines more frequently than teachers. They also express concern about the quality and suitability of information available on the Internet. Educators stress the importance of teaching students the skills to evaluate that information, since, at this point, the Internet does not impose standards equivalent to those of the publishing industry, or exercise the judgement of a school librarian.

Private Sector Partnerships

The growing emphasis on technology is fostering a new cooperation between education and industry. For example, New Brunswick has established a long-term partnership with both Apple and IBM for local area networking in the education system, and with Microsoft to create an interactive on-line "virtual campus," to provide students from K to 12 with courses not available at their own schools. Nova Scotia has received permission from a Boston company to use its Geoworks software, which brings older computers up to current standards with "window-like" capabilities.

New partnerships are also emerging as provincial departments of education and local school boards turn to the private sector for expertise and advice. For example, the Ontario Minister of Education and Training consulted with both educators and the private sector on the development of a comprehensive vision for the use of technology in K-12 classrooms, a five-year plan to achieve that vision, and an investment plan to support it. Alberta's Implementation Plan for

Technology in Education is based on two years of consultation with both educators and technical experts.

These partnerships with the private sector are not limited to technological developments, but they have been accelerated by them and welcomed by school systems which are short of human and financial resources. Some parents and educators question the trend, however, fearing that industry's view of students as potential consumers and employees is incompatible with the primary goals of public education.

School-to-Work Transitions

Every recent review of Canada's secondary schools has identified the need for improved co-ordination between school and work, especially for those students who do not proceed to college or university. Historically, traditional vocational programs have played an important role in preparing students for employment. However, since the 1960s, when post-secondary education became a realistic option for young people regardless of family income, such programs have lost their appeal. As a result, many young people graduate from secondary school with neither plans to pursue post-secondary education nor adequate job-skills to find employment.

Some provinces have taken specific action to address the needs of these students. In 1993, Quebec announced a major initiative to set up new vocational training programs in schools and in special school board vocational training centres. Alberta has introduced an Integrated Occupational Program for students at risk, giving them hands-on learning experience in areas like health care, the service industry, retailing trades and natural resources. Manitoba offers a variety of programs for youth aged 16-24 to facilitate the school-to-work transition, most designed to provide employment or entrepreneurial opportunities.

In the first integrated facility of its kind, the Integrated Centre for Industrial Mechanics in Beauce, Quebec, combines secondary school, college and university courses related to manufacturing. Each group educates at its own level using the same facilities and equipment: the school board trains future workers, Cégep Beauce-Appalaches prepares technicians, and the Université du Québec à Trois-Rivières involves researchers studying for their Masters Degrees.

The Nova Scotia Department of Education has entered into a $2.4 million cost-shared project agreement with Human Resources Development Canada to design and implement a three-year school-to-work transition pilot program in the public school system to facilitate the transition of students from high school to the workplace.

These examples illustrate a new emphasis on school-work transition at the high school level. In its 1996 publication, *School to Work Transitions: Changing Patterns and Research Needs*, HRDC identified a number of school-based responses found in schools and school boards across the country. It points out that these initiatives have been prompted by several factors, including a weak youth labour market, a growing concern about international competitiveness, and a recognition that institutional arrangements in other countries create fewer problems for students in making the transition from school to work.[4]

Mentoring, Career Counselling, and Job Placement Programs

Some school-work transition programs, like co-operative education and youth apprenticeships, include a formal "mentoring" relationship with adults, who take responsibility for assisting individual students in their job searches and adjustment to employment.

Career counselling has traditionally been part of the guidance program in secondary schools, and has focused on post-secondary options along with advice on résumé preparation, job search, and interview techniques.

In vocational schools, career counselling programs include job placement, either as part of work-experience programs for returning students or as post-graduation placement for graduating students.

School-Business Partnerships

The concept of school-business partnerships has been gaining popularity as a way of reducing drop-outs, increasing two-way communication between education and the private sector, and encouraging students to gain first-hand information about possible careers. In Canadian schools, the goal of these partnerships is not to provide specific employment opportunities for students, but to introduce them to the kinds of skills and attitudes required on the job. Activities include field trips to places of business, school visits from representatives of the workplace, industrial sabbaticals for teachers, curriculum development related to the operations of the business partner, mentorships, and provision of equipment and other resources to the school.

Despite the fact that these partnerships are increasing in number,

---

[4] The following material is summarized from: Harvey Krahn, *School to Work Transitions: Changing Patterns and Research Needs* (Ottawa: HRDC, 1996), pp. 47 - 52.

they are controversial among educators. Advocates argue that school-business partnerships help make curriculum more relevant to students and prepare them for the world of work. Critics suggest that such partnerships simply allow corporations to sell their ideas and products to students at a time when schools are badly in need of resources.

School-based Enterprises

In some schools, especially those with vocational programs, students operate school-based enterprises like restaurants, automobile repair shops, small factories, hair salons, newspapers, market gardens, and child care centres. These small businesses teach students a range of manual, clerical, business and public relations skills which they will need in future employment or as entrepreneurs.

Co-operative Vocational Education

Co-operative education gives high school students an opportunity to alternate between classroom learning and supervised work in a business or industrial setting. In some cases, it means a few weeks of work experience during a school term; in others, it involves a more structured, multi-year experience. In 1994, approximately 4% of Canadian high school students were participating in such programs, compared to 10% in the United States. Although co-operative education at the high school level has not been shown to make a measurable difference in post-graduation employment levels, it does provide students with a chance to "try out" a career idea, and an opportunity to learn workplace skills as part of their secondary school program.

Youth Apprenticeship Programs

Several provinces (including Ontario, Alberta, Manitoba and New Brunswick) have introduced youth apprenticeship programs at the high school level. Like traditional apprenticeship programs that are co-ordinated from post-secondary institutions, these high school-based programs include a mix of classroom instruction and practical, work-based training over several years. They may also include generic work skill and employment readiness training.

Youth apprentices enter into a contract with an employer, and are paid a low wage during their apprenticeship. Ontario's Youth Apprenticeship Program (OYAP) and Alberta's Registered Apprenticeship Program lead to formal trade certification; New Brunswick's Youth Apprenticeship Program provides participants with the opportunity to transfer into a formal apprenticeship.

Educational Trends

These programs appear promising as a response to school-work transition problems, but they are very costly, and relatively few employers have made themselves available for training. In addition, they continue to suffer from the second-class "vocational education" status. As a result, they have taken off slowly.

Trends in Post-secondary Education

The CMEC identified several areas of widespread activity in the post-secondary system, including renewal and articulation, accreditation of previous experience, and indicators of success.[5]

Efforts are under way across the country to re-focus universities and colleges in the face of declining resources. A number of provinces have established new bodies to oversee the renewal of post-secondary education, like Saskatchewan's Post-secondary Advisory Council. British Columbia has completed a strategic plan for post-secondary education, *Charting a New Course*, which establishes the future direction for the system, defines goals and objectives, and sets out strategies to meet them. Both within and between provinces, renewal efforts are focusing on articulation among institutions in an effort to reduce duplication and improve student access to post-secondary programs.

Related to articulation is the move to allow students to apply knowledge, wherever it has been acquired, to course credits at post-secondary institutions. This trend responds to both the need for greater equity and accessibility and the need for more efficient use of resources.

In a general move toward greater accountability, provinces and post-secondary institutions are developing indicators of success that can be used to demonstrate the effectiveness of their programs to potential students and to the public at large. Newfoundland is publishing a Post-secondary Indicator Report, the first performance report of its kind in Canada, based on follow-up surveys of graduates, needs assessments of special groups, and annual labour market sector studies.[6] Alberta has identified key performance indicators for its post-secondary institutions, and has introduced performance-based funds.

---

[5] CMEC, *Education Initiatives in Canada, 1996, op. cit.*, p. ii.
[6] *Ibid*, p. 4.

Trends in Skills Development and Training

CMEC also noted several trends in skills development and training programs across the country, including provincial and institutional reviews of existing programs in the light of the federal government's withdrawal from labour market training; an increased emphasis on employment preparation and skills training for social assistance recipients; partnerships between the post-secondary system and industry to deliver relevant skills; innovative community-based programs; and access to training through information technology.[7]

* * *

In democratic societies, educational systems reflect both existing social, economic, and political conditions and public expectations of how those conditions will change. As Canadians reach the end of the 20th century they are coping with shrinking resources, greater demands for accountability, new technologies, and a new work environment. These societal trends are having a profound impact on education in every jurisdiction and at every level, and they promise to keep Canadian education in a state of flux for the foreseeable future.

---

[7] *Ibid.*, pp. ii - iii.

Educational Trends

USEFUL ADDRESSES

Departments of Education

For general or detailed information about education in any particular province or territory, write to the department or ministry of education of the province or territory concerned. Or look them up on the world wide web.

Alberta — Department of Education, West Tower, Devonian Building, 11160 Jasper Avenue, Edmonton, Alberta T5K 0L2.
http://ednet.edc.gov.ab.ca

Department of Advanced Education and Career Development, 7th Floor, Commerce Place, 10155 - 102 Street, Edmonton, Alberta T5J 4L5
http://www.gov.ab.ca/dept/aecd.html

British Columbia — Ministry of Education, Skills and Training, Box 9156, Station Prov. Govt., Victoria, British Columbia V8W 9H2.
http://www.educ.gov.bc.ca

Manitoba — Department of Education and Training, Robert Fletcher Building, 1181 Portage Avenue, Winnipeg, Manitoba R3G 0T3.
http://www.mb.ca/educate/index.html

New Brunswick — Department of Education, P.O. Box 6000, Fredericton, New Brunswick E3B 5H1.
http://www.gov.nb.ca/education

Department of Advanced Education and Labour, P.O. Box 6000, Fredericton, New Brunswick E3B 5H1

Newfoundland and Labrador — Department of Education, 3rd Floor, Confederation Building, West Block, Box 8700, St. John's, Newfoundland A1B 4J6.
http://www.gov.nf.ca/edu/startedu.htm

Northwest Territories — Department of Education, Culture and Employment, (4501 - 50 Avenue), P.O. Box 1320, Yellowknife, Northwest Territories X1A 1L9.
http://siksik.learnnet.nt.ca/ece/default.html

Nova Scotia — Department of Education and Culture, Box 578, Halifax, Nova Scotia B3J 2S9.
http://www.ednet.ns.ca

Ontario — Ministry of Education and Training, Mowat Block, 900 Bay Street, Toronto, Ontario M7A 1L2. http://www.edu.gov.on.ca

Prince Edward Island — Department of Education (16 Fitzroy Street), Box 2000, Charlottetown, Prince Edward Island C1A 7N8.
http://www.gov.pe.ca/educ/index.html

Québec — Ministère de l'Éducation, Édifice Marie-Guyart, 11e étage, 1035, rue De La Chevrotière, Québec, Québec G1R 5A5.
http://www.meq.gouv.qc.ca

Saskatchewan — Department of Education, 2220 College Avenue, Regina, Saskatchewan S4P 3V7. http://www.gov.sk.ca/govt/educ

Department of Post-secondary Education and Skills Training, 2220 College Avenue, Regina Saskatchewan S4P 3V7.

Yukon — Department of Education, P.O. Box 2703, Whitehorse, Yukon Territory Y1A 2C6. http://www.yukonweb.wis.net/government

A Few Federal Addresses

Department of Canadian Heritage
Canadian Studies and Youth Programs

The programs this department undertakes have three components: support to the development of Canadian studies learning materials, youth participation, and the Terra Nova multi-media learning initiative.
Under the first program, the Department administers five funding programs to help the development costs for print, film, audio-visual and computer-based or computer-assisted Canadian studies learning materials.
The Youth Participation and Canadian studies programs have been combined to link learning about Canada and youth. Funding to cover part of the transportation costs is provided to national non-profit organizations that administer reciprocal group exchanges and national forums for young Canadians between the ages of 14 and 19.
The Terra Nova program assists in the financing and development of state-of-the-art Canadian learning and information products — CD-ROMS and material for distribution on electronic networks both in Canada and abroad. Materials are developed in partnership with multi-media software developers, educators, curricula developers, private sector interests and various levels of government.

General inquiries: (819) 997-0055
7th Floor, 15 Eddy Street, Jules Léger Building, Hull, QC K1A 0M5.
Fax: (819) 994-1314.

Department of Canadian Heritage
Citizens' Participation and Multiculturalism

Multiculturalism is part of the Citizenship and Canadian Identity Sector of the Department of Canadian Heritage whose objective is to foster a broader knowledge and appreciation of Canada, its values, symbols and institutions. Multiculturalism activities bring Canadians closer together, promote mutual respect among Canadians of different backgrounds, assist in the integration of first-generation Canadians, assist institutions to become more accessible and responsive to all Canadians, and promote harmonious inter-group and race relations.

11th Floor, 15 Eddy Street, Jules Léger Building, Hull QC K1A 0M5 Fax: (819) 953-9228.

Department of Canadian Heritage
Secretary of State - Official Languages Support Programs Branch

This branch administers the Official Languages in Education program which gives financial support to the provinces and territories to help defray additional costs in the operation and development of minority official language education and second official language instruction programs in elementary, secondary and post-secondary institutions. Financial support also includes the full financing of the Summer Language Bursary and the Official Language Monitor Programs, which are administered by the Council of Ministers of Education, Canada, in collaboration with the provinces and territories.
The branch also administers the Language Acquisition Development Program which provides direct financial help to voluntary organizations, professional associations and educational institutions for research or information projects on official languages in education.

15 Eddy Street, Jules Léger Building, Hull QC K1A 0M5 Fax: (819) 994-1917.

Department of Foreign Affairs and International Trade
International Academic Relations Division

This division encourages the development of teaching, research and publications about Canada in foreign universities. It offers awards tenable in Canada at the graduate level to foreign nationals under the Government of Canada Awards Program and the Canadian Commonwealth Scholarship and Fellowship Program. It also funds programs to encourage the study of Canada at universities abroad. It promotes the international sale of educational goods and services by assisting the marketing efforts of Canadian educational institutions. It facilitates international higher education contacts and co-operates with the Council of Ministers of Education, Canada, and private organizations to facilitate Canadian participation in international educational conferences and meetings.

Pearson Building, 125 Sussex Street, Ottawa, ON K1A 0G2. Tel: (613) 996-1014. Fax: (613) 992-5965. Web: http://www/dfait-maeci.gc.ca/english/culture.canstud.htm

Department of Health
Health Promotion and Programs Branch

This branch develops, promotes, supports and co-ordinates programs to preserve and advance physical and mental health of Canadians. Issues of nutrition, tobacco, alcohol, and drug use, AIDS, family health, cardiovascular disease and prevention of sexually transmitted diseases are addressed.

5th Floor, Jeanne Mance Building, Tunney's Pasture, Ottawa, ON K1A 0K9. Tel. (613) 954-8528 (communications). Fax: (613) 954-8529. Web: http://www.hwc.ca

Department of Indian Affairs and
Northern Development

Through its Indian Program Policy, this department is responsible for the education of status Indians and Inuit from primary through post-secondary levels.
Its Post-secondary Education Program provides grants to eligible students for tuition, travel and living costs for college and university studies and offers incentives, academic achievement and strategic studies scholarships. First Nations organizations currently administer over 90% of the Program through funding agreements with the department.

19th Floor, 10 Wellington Street, Hull QC K1A 0H4.
Tel: (613) 994-7431.   Fax: (613) 994-0443.
Web: http://www.inac.gc.ca

Department of National Defence
Dependants Education Program

Through its Dependants Education Program, this department operates a Canadian Curriculum section for elementary students at the AFCENT International School in Brunssum, Netherlands, serving the areas of Brunssum and of Geilenkirchen, Germany; and at SHAPE International School in Casteau, Belgium, serving that area. It also operates one degree-granting military college at Kingston, Ontario.

Major-General George R. Pearkes Building, Ottawa, ON K1A 0K2. Tel: (6) 992-3210. Fax: (613) 992-2073.

Human Resources Development Canada
Human Resources Investment Branch

This branch co-ordinates federal policies and programs related to education support. Through the Learning Directorate, the HRDC administers two main programs: the Post-secondary Education Financing Program, now under the Canada Health and Social Transfer (once the Established Program Financing) arrangements and the Canada Student Loans Program, which is administered in conjunction with provincial and territorial governments and financial institutions.

Phase IV, Place du Portage, 140 Promenade du Portage, Hull, QC K1A 0J9. Investment Branch - Fax: (819) 953-5603. Learning Directorate - Fax: (819) 997-0815.

Industry Canada
Science Promotion and Academic Affairs

This department is responsible for a number of education-related programs and projects.

SchoolNet facilitates the linkage of all Canada's 16,500 elementary and secondary schools and 3,400 public libraries to the information highway and makes national and international electronic educational resources available to Canadian teachers and students. Tel: (613) 993-5452. Fax: (613) 941-1296. Web: http://www.schoolnet.ca

Accessible through SchoolNet are *Virtual Products*, (databases, information and interactive experiences) that have been developed by, or in partnerships with, schools, colleges, universities, libraries and other educators. Tel: (613) 998-1331. Fax: (613) 941-2811.

SchoolNet Digital Collections is a program to help young Canadians develop high technology information management skills by transferring Canada's heritage, science and technology collections or materials from institutions across the country into digital form and putting them on SchoolNet. Tel: 1-800-465-7766. Fax: (819) 994-0576. Web: http://www.schoolnet.ca/collections

The Community Access Project (CAP) is an expansion of the SchoolNet program to help provide rural, small and remote communities with affordable public access to the Internet and the skills to use it. The program hopes to set up 1,500 centres across Canada by 1998. Local schools, libraries and selected community centres act as "on ramps" and provide training for individuals on how best to use the information highway. It is a joint endeavour of the federal, provincial and territorial governments. Tel: (613) 993-5690. Fax: (613) 952-8711. Web: http://www.cnet.unb.ca/cap

Computers for Schools helps schools and public libraries by channelling surplus computers and word processing software into classrooms and libraries across Canada. In partnership with provincial and territorial governments, business, communities, educators and volunteer groups, the program re-directs surplus computer equipment to help youth increase access to computers. It also provides hands-on repair training opportunities for youth at the program's refurbishment centres across the country. Tel: (613) 998-1804. Fax: (613) 957-1201.

Prime Minister's Awards for Teaching Excellence in Science, Technology and Mathematics. Industry Canada sponsors annual awards to honour teachers who have a proven impact on student performance and interest in science, technology and mathematics. The awards also go to teachers who best help students prepare for the knowledge-based economy (through problem-solving, teamwork and communication in the information technologies). Tel: (613) 957-9554. Fax: (613) 998-0943. Internet: pmawards@ic.gc.ca

C.D. Howe Building, 235 Queen Street, Ottawa, ON K1A 0H5. Tel: 1-800-268-6608.

Agencies

Canadian Commission for UNESCO

This body advises the federal government, through the Department of Foreign Affairs, on the UNESCO program and publicizes the work of UNESCO. It also provides liaison between UNESCO and Canadian agencies directly concerned with international co-operation in natural and social sciences, communications, education and cultural matters.

130 Albert Street, Box 1047, Ottawa, On K1P 5V8. Tel. (613) 566-4325. Fax (613) 566-4405.

Social Sciences and Humanities Research Council of Canada

This council promotes and assists research and scholarship in the social sciences and humanities. It supports independent research, helps in and facilitates the communication and exchange of research results. It administers programs of support for research and training in the social sciences and humanities, including research grants, scholarships and fellowships, and strategic grants.

350 Albert Street, P.O. Box 1610, Station B, Ottawa, ON K1P 6G4. Tel: (613) 992-0691.   Fax: (613) 992-1787.

Statistics Canada
Centre for Education Statistics

The Centre for Education Statistics stores, disseminates and analyzes national education statistics. Data are disseminated in a variety of forms (publications, microfiche, micro film, tapes and maps) and direct access to information is possible through CANSIM, Statistics Canada's machine readable database and retrieval system.

The Centre was established in collaboration with the provinces and territories, the Council of Ministers of Education, and the government of Canada, to develop a comprehensive program of pan-Canadian education statistics to support policy decisions and ensure that accurate information about education is available to the public.

R. H. Coats Building, Tunney's Pasture, Ottawa, ON K1A 0T6. Tel: (613) 951-1503. Fax: (613) 951-9040. Web: http://www.statcan.ca
Dissemination Division - Tel: 1-800-465-1222. Fax: (613) 951-4513.

National Education Organizations and Associations

Association of Canadian Community Colleges

The ACCC (founded in 1972) is a national voluntary association that represents colleges and technical institutes to government, business and industry, both in Canada and internationally. It acts with federal departments and agencies on members' behalf and links college capabilities to national industries. It also organizes conferences and workshops for its constituents.

Suite 200, 1223 Michael Street North, Ottawa, ON K1J 7T2. Tel: (613) 746-2222. Fax: (613) 746-6721. Web: http://www.accc.ca

Association canadienne d'éducation de langue française

ACELF (founded in 1947) is a national non-profit organization whose main objective is to promote and protect French language and culture in all francophone communities in Canada.
It serves as a clearinghouse, does research, acts as an agent for co-operation and training among francophone educators at all levels, parents and young people, school administrators, trustees and representatives of departments of education. It also publishes a magazine and a newsletter, directories and books on French language education in Canada.
It holds an annual convention and general meeting, seminars, profes-

sional development courses, and organizes student exchanges and a literary as well as a literacy program

268, rue Marie-de-l'Incarnation, Québec (QC) G1N 3G4. Tel: (418) 681-4661. Fax: (418) 681-3389. Web: http://www.acelf.ca

Association for Media and Technology in Education in Canada

AMTEC (founded in 1970) is a national association of educational technology professionals. All aspects of technology are dealt with by its members, including traditional audio-visual activities, film, television and computers. AMTEC produces a journal and conducts a comprehensive awards program. A highlight of its annual conference is the Media Festival Awards Banquet when awards for the year's outstanding media and computer productions are presented. The Association does not have a permanent secretariat address. A new president is elected each year from someone in the field.

Secretary-Treasurer: 3-1750 The Queensway, Suite 1318, Etobicoke, ON M9C 5H5.

Association of Universities and Colleges of Canada

The Association (AUCC), founded in 1911, fosters and promotes the interests of higher education in Canada and abroad. Degree-granting universities and colleges make up its membership and finance its core activities. The Association co-ordinates national and international initiatives undertaken by its member institutions and maintains a variety of centrally administered services. It represents the concerns of the university community to the Government of Canada, to the general public and at national and international forums.

Suite 600, 350 Albert Street Ottawa, ON K1R 1B1. Tel: (613) 563-1236. Fax: (613) 563-9745. Web: http://www.aucc.ca

Canadian Association for Distance Education

Established in 1983, CADE is a national association whose aim is to advance and promote research into distance education theory and practice. Its services include professional development, an annual conference, a journal published twice a year and a newsletter.

Suite 205, 1 Stewart Street, Ottawa, ON K1N 6H7. Tel: (613) 230-3630. Fax: (613) 230-2746. Web: http://www.cade-aced.ca

Canadian Association of School Administrators

CASA is a federation of a number of provincial affiliates. It promotes and provides support for its members' professional development. It assists its affiliates with provincial education issues and relates to national stakeholders to bring influence to policy matters at the federal level. It also promotes communication and liaison with national and international organizations with an interest in education.

Suite 405, 690 Dorval Drive, Oakville, ON L6K 3W7. Tel: (905) 845-2345; 1-888-212-5331. Fax: (905) 845-2044.

Canadian Association for University Continuing Education

CAUCE (founded in 1954) is a professional association of senior administrative personnel and practitioners whose professional careers are in university continuing education. Its objectives include the dissemination of information about university continuing education personnel and programs, the professional development of those working in the field, the recognition of meritorious achievement of both institutions and individuals, the representation of university continuing education in Canada (including liaison with government departments, other national associations and organizations outside Canada), and the promotion and support of research and policy studies into the practice and management of continuing education.

Suite 600, 350 Albert St., Ottawa, ON 1B1. Tel: (613) 563-1236. Fax: (613) 563-773.

Canadian Bureau for International Education

The CBIE's membership includes post-secondary institutions, individuals and national and local organizations involved with education. The bureau administers education travel and exchange programs. It acts as a resource centre for foreign student advisors on Canadian campuses and it maintains contact with federal and provincial governments to express its views and those of its constituency on policies that affect foreign students in Canada. CBIE also contracts to place foreign students in Canadian institutions.

Suite 1100, 220 Laurier Avenue West, Ottawa, ON K1P 5Z9. Tel: (613) 237-4820. Fax: (613) 237-1073. Web: http://www.cbie.ca

Canadian Council for Exceptional Children

The purpose of this council is to advance the general welfare and education of all exceptional children and youth in Canada and to disseminate information about exceptional children. The CCEC co-ordinates the work of its units, supports the publication of a journal in special education and co-operates with other Canadian agencies and organizations concerned with exceptional children to conduct studies and publish reports.

1010 Polytek Court, Unit 36, Gloucester, ON K1J 9J2. Tel: (613) 747-9226. Fax: (613) 745-9282.

Canadian Education Association

The CEA (founded in 1891) is a non-political bilingual organization whose central objective is promoting the improvement of education. The Association serves as a common meeting place for all sectors of education through its professional development activities, meetings, conventions and special projects. It also is a central source of information on education in Canada for the education community and the general public.
The Association produces documents that include a directory of

names and addresses of people in education (the *CEA Handbook*), the *Newsletter*, and its French counterpart *Le Bulletin*, a magazine *Education Canada*, and publications on topics of current concern. Its information gathering and sharing services include a Quick Query service for members and an Information Plus Service for more in-depth analysis and summaries.

Suite 8-200, 252 Bloor Street West, Toronto, ON M5S 1V5.
Tel: (416) 924-7721. Fax: (416) 924-3188. Web: http://www.acea.ca

Canadian Guidance and Counselling Association

The CGCA is a national professional association of persons in guidance and counselling education, business and industry, public service agencies and government. It works towards the development and co-ordination of existing guidance and counselling services as well as towards improving conditions, resources, research and facilities for guidance and counselling.

Suite 600, 220 Laurier Avenue West, Ottawa, ON K1P 5Z9. Tel: (613) 230-4236. Fax: (613) 230-5884.

Canadian Home and School Federation

The CHSF (founded in 1927) is a federation of provincial and local parent-teacher groups composed of people whose goals are to promote the welfare of children and youth, raise the standard of home life, foster co-operation between parents and teachers, encourage high ideals of citizenship and promote, by educational means, international goodwill and peace.

Suite 104, 858 Bank Street, Ottawa, ON K1S 3W3. Tel: (613) 234-7292. Fax: (613) 234-3913. Web: http://cnet.unb.ca/cap/partners/chsptf

Canadian School Boards Association

The CSBA (founded in 1923) is the national voice of the provincial associations of school boards and school trustees. CSBA comprises nine provincial school board associations representing over 400 school boards. It promotes educational excellence as a national imperative, provides leadership on issues with national importance and fosters and promotes local autonomy in education. CSBA believes in public education that is both accessible and universal and governance by locally elected school boards.

Suite 350, 130 Slater Street, Ottawa, ON K1P 6E2. Tel: (613) 235-3724. Fax: (613) 238-8434. admin@cdnsba.org Web: http://www.cdnsba.org

Canadian Society for the Study of Education

The primary objective of CSSE (founded in 1972) is to promote the advancement of research in education throughout Canada. The Society provides a forum for scholarly debate through its publications and annual conferences and contributes to scholarly exchange among the members of its affiliated associations.
Its co-operating associations, all of which retain their identity within the CSSE, are the Canadian Association for Curriculum Studies, Canadian Association of Deans of Education, Association francophone des doyennes et des doyens, des directeurs and des directrices d'éducation, Canadian Association for Educational Psychology, Canadian Association for Foundations of Education, Canadian Association for the Study of Educational Administration, Canadian Association for the Study of Women in Education, Canadian Association for Teacher Education, Canadian Educational Researchers Association, and the Comparative and International Education Society of Canada.

Suite 205, 1 Stewart Avenue, Ottawa, ON K1N 6H7.
Tel: (613) 230-3532. Fax: (613) 230-2746.

Canadian Society for the Study of Higher Education

The CSSHE (formed in 1970) provides communication among persons in academic disciplines and administrative positions conducting or using research in post-secondary education. Its purpose is the advancement of knowledge in post-secondary education through research and the dissemination of the results in publications and learned meetings. The Society publishes a journal, holds an annual conference, co-operates in the publication of special studies and makes recommendations on developmental policy in higher education to government.

Suite 320, 350 Albert Street, Ottawa, ON K1R 1B1. Tel: (613) 563-1236. Fax: (613) 563-7739.

Canadian Teachers' Federation

The CTF (founded in 1920) receives its support from the provincial and territorial teacher organizations. It publishes reports and studies, sponsors seminars on matters of professional concern, provides an information service and represents the interests of teachers at the national and international levels. CTF is a member of Education International.

110 Argyle Avenue, Ottawa, ON K2P 1B4. Tel: (613) 232-1505. Fax: (613) 232-1886. Web: http://www.ctf-fce.ca

Council of Ministers of Education, Canada

The Council of Ministers of Education, Canada (CMEC), formed in 1967, is a national council of provincial and territorial ministers responsible for education. It was set up as a forum for consultation and exchange of information on national policy issues in education. The Council also facilitates a broad range of co-operative activities among the provinces at the elementary, secondary and post-secondary levels. It also facilitates interprovincial consultation on education-related matters that involve the federal government. This includes arranging for the participation of provincial authorities in international conferences and exchanges.

Suite 5-200, 252 Bloor Street West, Toronto, ON M5S 1V5. Tel: (416) 964-2551. Fax: (416) 964-2296. Web: http://www.cmec.ca

Federation of Independent Schools in Canada

The FISC, founded in 1980, acts on behalf of provincial and national independent (private) school associations. The Federation's objectives include the maintenance of comprehensive resource documents on independent schools that include the names of provincial and national contact persons, provincial regulations across Canada, provincial and national activities and major issues.

9125 - 50th Street, Edmonton, AB   Tel: (403) 469-9868. Fax: (403) 469-9880. E-mail: (gduthler@kingsu.ab.ca)